THE CLOUDS REMEMBER

THE F.2A FLYING BOAT

The
CLOUDS REMEMBER

The Aeroplanes of World War I

By

LEONARD   BRIDGMAN

*

With a commentary by
OLIVER   STEWART, M.C., A.F.C.

Arms and Armour Press

This edition first published in 1972 by
Arms and Armour Press
Lionel Leventhal Limited,
2-6 Hampstead High Street,
London, N.W.3

SBN 85368 079 5

The publishers are pleased to acknowledge the
assistance of the Imperial War Museum in
making possible this edition, reproduced from
the original volume published in 1936 by Gale & Polden

Reprinted in England by Kingprint Limited,
Orchard Road, Richmond, Surrey.

PREFACE

" As the waves after ebb drawing seaward,
When the hollows are full of the night,
So the birds that flew singing to me-ward
Recede out of sight." (Swinburne)

AVIATION approaches maturity. It is settling down to a routine
of existence, and whether the future brings peace or war, it is not
likely again to see a period of adventure and effort like that which
we look upon in these pages. It was a period rich in courage.
Aeroplane designers and pilots were exploring in unknown regions.
They had no charts of experience and accumulated scientific data
to guide them. They were obliged to trust largely to their sense
of direction, their creative instinct and to seek in their own minds
and with their own hands for solutions to the problems of flight.

That is one reason why the aeroplanes with which we concern
ourselves in this volume must always possess interest. They are
individuals and pioneers, born from the strivings of the creative
mind. Many of them are bursting with originality and with
independent ideas. None of them falls into any standardized
group to be dismissed as " typical." In the general design and in
the detail design there is evidence of the desperate struggles in
which the artist-engineers of that time so enthusiastically engaged.

To-day, it may be supposed, the creators of modern aeroplanes
would be insulted if they were called " artist-engineers." They
are " engineers " *tout court*. Even those who have worked right
through from the beginning of flying and are still working now
would disclaim artistic abilities with a scornful curling of the lip.
Because to-day the creation of an aeroplane design is not the task
of one man, or of ten men, or of twenty men, it is the task of thousands of men. It consists in the selective application of knowledge
from the great mass collected over a period of years by innumerable
workers in many different researches. In the artistic sense an
aeroplane is no longer " created "—it is assembled.

That change has added something to the aeroplane and it has
taken something away. The performance of the modern aeroplane
is better and is more accurately predictable ; faults are less likely
to reveal themselves in flight. All aeroplanes designed for the

same duty will be much the same ; the methods of construction will be similar ; the overall shape will be similar ; the performance will be similar and, finally, the flying qualities will be similar. Hearing an announcement of a new aeroplane we no longer expect to be surprised by some startling innovation or some astonishing break-away from convention. Knowing the duty, we can almost guess the formula.

The days of the introduction of new machines like the D.H.2, the Sopwith triplane, the Morane Parasol, the Vickers Vampire, the Bat Bantam, the Westland Pterodactyl and the Cierva Autogiro, if not entirely over, are on the wane. The like of those flashes of mechanical genius, the Gnôme and the Monosoupape, engines which no pure " engineer " could have invented, because they arose from the daring which reaches out beyond mathematics into the field of artistic creation, and that jewel the 80 h.p. Le Rhône, will not be seen again. If some unorthodox type of engine or aeroplane does occasionally appear, it will not be likely to last long enough to establish itself in general service and to become known to scores of pilots. Yet that was what some of the unorthodox types of the past succeeded in doing.

They created a stir by their originality and newness when they first appeared, and they came into service and were known to and flown by many pilots. The spectacle of the extraordinary becoming the ordinary was common. Machines which might have merited the name of freak when they first appeared were built and used in such large numbers that they finally came to be accepted as perfectly normal.

Reference works exist which give the dimensions, structural methods and performance of these aeroplanes and engines, but so far as we know no attempt has previously been made to seize and set down the imponderable qualities by which pilots knew and recognized them—to interpret them through their manners and looks. That is what we try to do here. We try to give a little more than photographs and figures, machine drawings and mathematical data can give, we try to put them in the air once more and to present them in action.

It is a picture extraordinarily difficult to get down on paper ; a picture compact of sights, sounds and scents. We do not claim that it has the historical importance of statistical data any more than that the details of the armour worn in the battles of the past have the importance of the descriptions of the battles ; but we claim that it is not entirely without value, and that it may have an interest of its own.

For those aeroplanes were fascinating machines in spite of—or perhaps because of—their often uncertain behaviour. Their incalculable qualities showed in them as in an attractive woman, and enhanced their interest. They were rich in extremes and opposites ; they were unexpected, dangerous, difficult, strange, beautiful, comic, vicious—but they were never dull. By means of the pictures in these pages and the text accompanying them we try to convey the essential " look " and " touch " and " flavour " of the aeroplanes belonging to what might, without straining the point, be called the heroic period of aeronautical development, a period extending from the beginning to the time in 1937 when large-scale mass production of types conforming to the modern formula began.

Around each machine is built up some sort of character study in the effort to convey the kind of responses it gave when it was in flight and to enable the reader to understand it and even to take over the controls. Flying qualities in the period with which we deal varied enormously, and contemporary judgments were often curious. The pilot held a higher position as critic than he does to-day, and the reputations of aeroplanes were made or marred by what the pilots who flew them said about them. Handling trials consisted of aerobatics of any kind the pilot chose to perform.

It might be thought that these aeroplanes, into which went so much thought and so much invention, were therefore at the mercy of prejudice, for there is nobody more prejudiced than the average aeroplane pilot. But the demands of warfare seemed to act as a corrective to prejudice. Some good aeroplanes were " killed " before they reached the squadrons ; but that was usually as a result of staff decisions and not as a result of pilots' reports. The Bristol monoplane provides an example of the way the opinions of pilots were over-ridden by staff officers, for the machine was never adopted for the Royal Flying Corps, although it was highly thought of by those who had flown it. An academic point about poor outlook was offered as the reason for its rejection.

The reactions of pilots to aeroplanes which were dangerous were the same then as they are now. Pilots who had flown the type and lived would go about saying that the stories of its viciousness were nonsense. You had but to fly it thus and thus, they would explain, and it was perfectly safe. To-day, pilots who have not experienced ice-formation suggest that its prevalence has been much exaggerated. It is probably true to say that only a pilot with fairly extensive testing experience and a familiarity with a large number of different types could hope to give an unbiased opinion about the qualities of an aeroplane.

The Sopwith Camel, for instance, although it killed many people, evoked fanatic loyalty from those who flew it. Camel pilots were excessively proud of being Camel pilots, and the aeroplane acquired by a sort of reflection many of those virtues which its pilot secretly attributed to himself. Camels made conversation in many Royal Flying Corps and Royal Naval Air Service messes for a long time. They were almost universally looked up to as being something special. Yet now that we can look at the Camel unswayed by its war-time glamour, with the soberer judgment of the years, we must admit that it was in fact a treacherous aeroplane—one-sided, feverish, vicious. To exchange the Sopwith Snipe, which followed it, for the Camel was to exchange the " lilies and languors of virtue for the roses and raptures of vice."

Partly because it was vicious it gained much respect. But even at this remove we must also realize that the Camel had one quality in supreme degree, a quality which at that time was looked upon as being of the highest importance in fighting in the air—it had the power of lightning manœuvre. With the possible exception of the Bat Bantam, it seems probable that the Camel remains to this day the most highly manœuvrable machine that has ever existed. It had a hair-trigger elevator and ailerons which felt as if they were capable of rolling the wings off the fuselage.

Those who study the pictures and the text in this volume will, we hope, obtain more than the matter and measurements which went to make up these aeroplanes, more than the millimetres and miles an hour, more than the tin and timber ; they will see the aeroplanes themselves and will notice, perhaps, a faint flavour of what the pilots felt who handled them. Aeroplanes of 1938, with their metal stressed-skin construction and their 1,000 h.p. engines are pantechnicons to the small frail machines of the war period and the immediate post-war period. Aeroplanes like the Bristol Scout and the Sopwith Pup and, later, the Sopwith Snail and the Westland Wagtail, resembled D. H. Lawrence's mosquito, that " translucent phantom shred of a frail corpus," incredibly fine and light, yet able, like the mosquito, to command attention.

Machinery is responsible for a good deal of pseudo-mystic meandering. We have Honegger trying to translate a locomotive into music ; we have Rupert Brooke's " passionless beauty of a great machine " ; we have Stephen Spender with " The Express " (" After the first powerful plain manifesto, the black statement of pistons . . .") ; we have almost every writer of recent years trying to squeeze human connotations out of the machine. Occasionally this is straining after effects that are not there. The driver of a motor-car, the helmsman of a ship, the pilot of an aeroplane must put forth an effort of the imagination if he is to confer upon his machine his own sort of consciousness. But, hemmed in by machines, man probably tries to make the best of them by persuading himself that they have something human about them, a sort of semi-consciousness.

It is a delusion, but an expedient one. And it may contain a particle of fact. The machine, although possessing no real personality of its own, may reflect back parts of the personality of the man in charge of it. It is noteworthy that the expert pilot always wants to fly the aeroplane which is rumoured to be difficult and dangerous. It challenges his skill and reflects his own confidence in his skill when he flies it. In the end he feels affectionately towards it. We shall not strain after personalities in these aeroplanes, but we shall hope to give some idea of the subjective impressions of the pilots. These impressions were in part the outcome, not only of personal experience at the controls, but also of an elaborate and involved tissue of rumours, stories, gossip. All aeroplanes have been subject to this superimposed comment. When a new aeroplane is designed rumours begin to circulate. It is said that it will be capable of unheard-of speeds ; that it will be supremely manœuvrable, or that it will have a tremendous rate of climb.

Later, when it flies, other rumours will spread. Its ailerons, the word will run, are utterly useless. You can move the stick from side to side and nothing will happen—nothing at all. Or it has " no elevator," or it stalls suddenly on right-hand turns, or it spins at the least provocation, or it is stable on its back and if it is flown upside down it cannot be righted again, or it cannot be extricated from a spin.

The sum total of the aeroplane's reputation is affected by all this kind of chatter, and in these pages we shall not hesitate to allude to such common gossip where it seems to contribute to an understanding of the machine and of the part it played. Most of the aeroplanes dealt with are no longer capable of bringing libel actions, so we shall be secure in telling what we know about them, even to the sometimes ill-informed gossip which occasionally affected their progress.

It has been mentioned that this is not intended to be a list of data or a collection of statistics. Performance and other figures, as they usually help in providing a full understanding of an aeroplane, are frequently given, but throughout we have tried to keep in view our main objectives, to re-create the aeroplanes which played the chief parts in aeronautical development, not as they are in the workshop, but as they are in the air ; to set them in their

right perspective relative to general progress, and to provide
through the medium of these " abrupt and charming movers," a
slight side-note to aeronautical history.

One caution must be uttered about the figures given. These
are usually the official figures, although sometimes they are manufacturers' figures. It is well known that large differences, which
may be as much as 10 per cent., occur in the performance in
speed and climb obtained by aeroplanes in service in the squadrons
compared with the prototypes. The difference may be up or
down, but that it frequently exists is beyond dispute. It is also
noteworthy that aeroplanes used often to be modified without
being renamed and in consequence performance again varied.
It becomes impossible to fix a definite performance on a definite
aeroplane. But, although no claim for finality can be made for
the data in this book, an attempt has been made to obtain trustworthy evidence as to performance from those best entitled to
give it and we offer our thanks to those manufacturers and test
pilots who have given their assistance.

Turn now, in Stephen Spender's words, to " the streamers
of white cloud and whispers of wind in the listening sky," and
to those flying machines which " travelled a short while towards
the sun and left the vivid air signed with their honour."

CONTENTS

CONTENTS

ILLUSTRATIONS

xiii

R.F.C. BLÉRIOT 1913 MILITARY TRIALS TYPE

THE BLÉRIOT MONOPLANE

To M. Louis Blériot belongs the distinction of being the pioneer aviator who saw farthest into the future. Apart from C. Ader the Wright Brothers are regarded as having been the first to achieve man-controlled flight, but Blériot was the first to sketch out in a full-scale machine the shape of the aeroplane of the future. When most people were pinning their faith to the biplane ; when most of the successful flights were being done by biplanes, from the performances of the Wright Brothers to those of Mr. Henry Farman in a Voisin, Blériot chose the monoplane.

His was the inspiration of genius, and the depth of that inspiration can be gauged by examining the R.F.C. two-seater Blériot monoplane, No. 221, depicted by Leonard Bridgman. It has nothing of the clumsiness, the queerness, the top-heaviness of the biplanes of its time. To the eyes of the pilot of to-day, accustomed to the cleaned-up, streamline monoplanes which have been evolved as a result of the intensive labours of thousands of scientists, experimenters and designers, the old Blériot monoplane still looks handsome. Unlike some of the early biplanes it does not tend to provoke superior laughter.

M. Blériot not only figured as an inspired designer, but also as an inspired pilot. He had many crashes, but he was never discouraged, and in 1908 he made what has been described as the first genuine cross-country flight on record. It was from Toury to Artenay, a distance of 14 kilometres, and he did the flight in 11 minutes. But the feat which is best remembered, and which immediately springs to mind when one looks upon a picture of the old Blériot monoplane, is the Channel crossing of the 25th July, 1909. It was accomplished by a single-seater machine.

In 1908 Farman had won a money prize by making a 1,000 yards circuit, and when Lord Northcliffe offered a money prize for the first aeroplane flight across the English Channel, Blériot made arrangements to attempt to win it. Just before he set out Hubert Latham had made his historic, but unsuccessful attempt. Blériot's cross-channel machine had the 25 h.p. three-cylinder Anzani, forerunner of the modern air-cooled radial engine, so that the little monoplane may be said on that occasion to have brought to

B   I

England not only the 1937 conception of the aeroplane, but also of the aero-engine.

The few moments before Blériot set off have been described again and again, and his famous remark to Leblanc, " Where is Dover ? " and the reply, with a vague wave of the hand, " It's over there," have become almost legendary. Certain it is that Blériot had no compass and no clock. In place of the modern radio equipment, turn and bank indicator, fore-and-aft level, automatic pilot and course and distance calculator, he had the smoke of the French destroyer *Escopette*. But he had soon passed that, and for about ten minutes he was out of sight of land and shipping. It must have been good fortune as much as anything else which enabled him to keep approximately on his course. Actually he departed from it a little and came over English soil at St. Margaret's Bay. He made his landing at Dover Castle Cliff, where a tablet commemorates the achievement. His time in the air had been about 40 minutes and his speed approximately 45 m.p.h., a speed which the Chief Coastguard at Dover, who had seen the machine in the air, described as " almost incredible."

Thereafter the Blériot monoplane went through a process common to all successful aeroplanes. It was fitted with successively more powerful engines ; it was altered here and there ; but its general plan did not alter. With a wing span of 28 ft. 3 in., a length of 23 ft., a wing area of 150 sq. ft. and a chord of 6 ft. 6 in., the cross-channel Blériot possessed several features of more than passing interest. The undercarriage was of the swivelling wheel type, and the early machines had a tail-wheel. The theory behind this undercarriage was that an aeroplane might, through changes in wind direction at the moment of landing, touch the ground with a certain amount of drift. The castoring wheels could deal with this drift. Actually it was found that too much importance had been attached to the loads set up by any possible drift at landing ; but the undercarriage provides an indication of how thoroughly the various practical problems of flight had been studied.

The cross-channel machine forecast the flotation gear now used in the aeroplanes of the Fleet Air Arm, for behind the pilot's seat, in the after-part of the fuselage, a bag inflated with air was carried. The airscrew was made by Chauvière and was of 6 ft. 8 in. diameter, and the all-up weight, including the pilot, was 660 lb. Lateral control was by warping the wings, and the rudder was controlled by pedals. The elevator had an area of 16 sq. ft.

It should be mentioned, too, that the Anzani engine was controlled by the ignition advance and retard mechanism, as were the engines of many of the early motor-cars. The inlet valves were automatic and the exhaust valves mechanically operated. They were at the sides of the cylinders. The next engine to be fitted to the Blériot monoplane after the Anzani was the British E.N.V., which was an eight-cylinder V-type engine of 50 h.p., and after that came the Gnôme and with it a further increase in speed.

At the Doncaster meeting of 1909 M. Delagrange achieved an officially observed speed of 49·9 m.p.h. with his Gnôme-engined Blériot, and this was received as a world's record, though whether the claim was justified is not known. At any rate, the Blériot on this account and also possibly on account of the " almost incredible " speed observed by the Dover coastguard, acquired a reputation for being extremely fast and the monoplane form was regarded by some as essentially the " racing " form of aeroplane, a thing which probably held back its development in other directions.

Although a view of the old Blériot monoplane recalls above all else the crossing of the English Channel—and it is to be remembered that it did not only the first flight across it, but also the second, in the hands of M. de Lesseps—yet from the severely aerodynamical point of view it is probable that the Blériot's greatest contribution to aviation was the way it revealed the possibilities of aircraft control. It was the first aeroplane to be used for stunting or aerobatics, and the machine was so manœuvrable that, in those early days, it was made to do nearly all the aerobatics ever invented. With the exception of one or two manœuvres it completely covered the ground. The introduction of the Camel, the supreme aerobatic aeroplane, only served to give the stunts which the Blériot had originated rather greater vividness and rather more spectacular interest.

After the Blériot had established itself as a machine with a remarkably good performance by making a world's duration record of 5 hours 3 minutes and $5\frac{1}{3}$ seconds at the 1910 Reims meeting in the hands of M. Olieslagers ; by obtaining first place in the general classification at the 1910 Bournemouth meeting in the hands of M. L. F. Morane, with a speed of 56 m.p.h. and a climb to 4,107 ft. in under 17 minutes ; by setting up a new speed record of 77·67 m.p.h. in the hands of James Radley at Lanark in the same year ; and by setting up an altitude record of 10,746 ft. at Pau flown by M. G. Legagneux, it came into the hands of that genius among pilots, Emile Pégoud.

In various forms the Blériot had been used by " Beaumont," Gordon Bell, Hucks, Salmet and Gustav Hamel. It had won the 1911 Circuit d'Europe ; it had established in 1911 a record for distance in a straight line, the course being London to Paris, and the pilot M. Pierre Prier, and a record for height with 13,943 ft., the pilot being M. Roland Garros. All these records were made with the Gnôme engine. It had also been the subject of continuous development work by M. Blériot who, in 1912, published his report on certain accidents to the French Government, in which he stated for the first time the theory of downloads on the wings. It had survived the idiotic ban on monoplanes issued by the British Secretary of State for War in 1912.

But until Pégoud performed his amazing feats, no advanced aerobatics had been invented. There had been the *vol plané*, straight, in a spiral and with S-turns, and there had been the *vol piqué* in which Hamel and Hucks specialized. Then news reached England of Pégoud's performance. In a Blériot monoplane he was said to have " looped the loop " at Juvisy on the 1st September, 1913. British pilots refused to believe the truth of the reports. Further news came through. Pégoud had become in France a national hero and was cheered wherever he went. His flying became more and more daring. Finally Pégoud was persuaded to come to Brooklands with his Blériot.

On the 25th, 26th and 27th September, 1913, Pégoud amazed everyone interested in aviation in Great Britain by his display. Some say that a Russian pilot was the first to do a loop in an aeroplane ; and it may be true that somebody or other made a loop before Pégoud, but indubitably Pégoud was the first man to loop deliberately and understandingly as he was indubitably the first to perform innumerable other aerobatics, including the bunt, and feats of daring, including a leap from an aeroplane in mid air and descent by parachute.

Pégoud is too little regarded in the history of flying, possibly because he was so far ahead of his day as an executant. He did more to develop and amass experience of the handling qualities of aeroplanes than anybody else. His first aerobatic at Brooklands was one which to-day, twenty-five years after, would still provoke wonder and applause if it were done at the Royal Air Force Display. It was the vertical " S." Pégoud put the nose of his Blériot down and forced the stick forward until he had completed a bunt and the machine was flying inverted ; he then pulled the stick back again and pulled out in a dive.

He also tail-slid—a manœuvre seen only on the rarest occasions nowadays and generally regarded by modern pilots as dangerous— and he half-rolled. He also half-rolled from the top of a loop, and he developed upside-down flying and in 1913 was doing periods of one and a half minutes upside down, with engine on, making turns to right and left. The flights were made under the supervision of Louis Blériot who specially strengthened the machine to meet what he calculated would be the additional loads.

Among the specially introduced strengthening features was a special cabane above the pilot's head which enabled the landing wires to the wings to be set at a rather more favourable angle. The tail of the machine was also altered with the object of giving greater control. In other respects the aeroplane used by Pégoud, the one which made the first series of deliberate advanced aerobatics, was the same as that illustrated by Leonard Bridgman. Pégoud's parachute jump had also been done from a Blériot in August, 1913.

This was one with a five-cylinder Anzani engine. The parachute was of the type that opened while the pilot was still in the aeroplane, and it was intended to lift him out of his seat. Not many pilots would agree to try a device of that kind to-day with all the knowledge of parachutes and aircraft that has been added since Pégoud's experiment. But Pégoud's courage was matchless ; he took off in the old Blériot, climbed to 700 feet, shut off the engine and pulled the parachute release. Pégoud was lifted from his seat and deposited in a tree, while the old Blériot, after turning on its back, righted itself and glided down and made quite a good landing in a field.

Probably Pégoud's greatest contribution to aviation was psychological. At a time when unknown fears of " what might happen " constantly menaced the air pilot, Pégoud found out and showed what *did* happen, and demonstrated that it was not so terrible after all. He showed that a well-found machine, such as the Blériot, could be extricated by a pilot from every possible position provided there was sufficient height. The terrors which pilots had imagined were shown to be non-existent. Aeroplane flying was put on a rational basis and men were given their biggest impetus towards full mastery of the machine.

In my opinion—and I admit it is a personal opinion not shared by many—no greater air pilot has ever lived than Pégoud. He was a pioneer in a field even more difficult than those of speed and distance, because so little was known about it. And to realize just how much Pégoud did, it is only necessary to watch a modern display of aerobatics. There will be nothing there except the spin and variations of the spin, such as the falling leaf and the flick roll, that Pégoud did not do. The multiplication of engine power has enabled certain things to be put together to form manœuvres which are called " new," but in fact they are made up of the elements discovered by Pégoud. The " spectacles " or figure of eight lying on its side, for instance, is a mixture of loop and bunt made possible by appropriate engine power.

After Pégoud many other pilots took to aerobatics. B. C. Hucks specialized in upside-down flying and gave many displays in his specially strengthened Blériot at Hendon and in other parts of the country. Marcus D. Manton performed the bunt and the Blériot, after being described as a " racing " machine, became also a " stunting " machine. In fact, by now this remarkable monoplane had shown itself to be master of the whole range of aeronautics. It had achieved speed, distance and height records and it had demonstrated handling qualities of a remarkably high order.

In August, 1914, it went to war in large numbers in the air services of France and Great Britain and Blériot pilots and observers, armed with rifles and revolvers and provided with primitive wireless sets, hand grenades, etc., laid the foundations of air reconnaissance in those critical early months of the War.

A great original, it is probable that no matter how far aviation develops in the future, how brilliant the new discoveries and the new designs, the aeroplanes will for ever bear evidence of the debt they owe to Louis Blériot and the Blériot monoplane.

THE MAURICE FARMAN LONGHORN

To the large numbers of pilots who joined the Royal Flying Corps during the early part of the War, the wires and wood, the front elevator—that disembodied control surface—and the " spectacles " of the Maurice Farman Longhorn will be strongly evocative. The sight of one of these machines, the early antithesis of the " cleaned up " monoplane, a design opposite to the Blériot and the Morane, is reminiscent of two-gallon petrol cans, crash hats and the mystery and mumbo-jumbo of early aviation.

Judged upon present-day standards, the Maurice Farman Longhorn, unlike the Blériot and Morane monoplanes, was " all wrong." A mass of wires and struts, there was no apparent attempt to produce a streamline or near-streamline machine. Nothing was prophetic about the Longhorn—provided always that the remarkable 70 h.p. Renault engine be excluded. The aeroplane was an example of a thing that flew in spite of, and not because of, aerodynamic theory.

And it flew well. Look back on the history of the Maurice Farman. In 1910 it set up a distance record on a closed circuit of 350 miles. The pilot was M. Tabuteau and the place Buc. Then it held for the three subsequent years the world's duration record. In 1911, the time in the air was 11 hours 1 minute and $29\frac{1}{2}$ seconds, and in 1912 and 1913 it was 13 hours 22 minutes. The pilot was M. Fourny. The Maurice Farman was exhibited at the 1911 Aero Show and it took part in the Laffan's Plain review on the King's birthday. There were six Maurice Farmans in the military wing on this occasion.

Still more noteworthy were the Maurice Farman achievements in competitions and races. In the military trials of 1912 the Maurice Farman took part, but unfortunately the tests included a timed dismantling and assembly test. Anyone who has taken one look at a Maurice Farman will know what this means, and the four mechanics who dismantled the military trials Maurice Farman and reassembled it, working against the clock, deserve to be ranked among the true heroes of aviation. They took only 1 hour 18 minutes to dismantle it and only 3 hours 16 minutes to reassemble it—an astonishing feat.

7

THE MAURICE FARMAN LONGHORN

In this same year of 1912, M. Pierre Verrier, who made a name as one of the best Longhorn pilots, flew one of these machines in the Aerial Derby. He took advantage of the curious tiered seating arrangement (echoed later in the big F.Es.) to strap his map to his own back and to call upon his passenger to read it and tell him which way to go. Whether this method proved unsatisfactory, or for some other reason, Verrier lost his way. It was in 1912, too, that Verrier made a flight during a gale. The wind was gusting at least up to 50 m.p.h. when Verrier took off in his Maurice Farman to fly from Hendon to Brooklands.

The bumps did their best against the multitudinous wires and struts which were presented to them, but Verrier plugged along and, after an interminable period in the air, landed at Brooklands. His average speed worked out at nine miles an hour. Then there was the London to Manchester race entry of J. Alcock, a name afterwards to be inscribed deeply in aeronautical history. The Maurice Farman Longhorn flown by Alcock on this occasion was British-built and it was fitted with a British engine, a 100 h.p. Sunbeam. The machine showed a turn of speed, if the phrase may be permitted in relation to a Longhorn, but a delay at the start prevented it from effective participation in the race.

Then there was the night racing at Hendon in 1913, a bold and successful experiment. Louis Noël flew the Maurice Farman on this occasion. Noël became well known as a pilot of these machines and he and Verrier were perhaps their chief exponents in England. The Longhorn was the aeroplane which was responsible for more of those harrowing articles entitled " My First Flight in an Aeroplane " than any other machine, for it was a prodigiously successful passenger-carrier and its top speed of 55 to 57 m.p.h. was ample, in those days, to give those who flew in it the chance of discussing the thrills of high-speed travel.

The present writer learned to fly in a Maurice Farman Longhorn. His experiences may have resembled those of many other Royal Flying Corps pilots who made their first solo after less than two hours' instruction. The pupil sat behind and above his instructor, with his feet on either side of him and, leaning over and around him, he placed his hands on the " spectacles," over the hands of the instructor. As for rudder bars or rudder pedals, those were left to the instructor, and the method of using them was left to the inherited aptitude—if any—of the pupil. It was a pleasing experience thus to circle the aerodrome, perched up above and behind one's instructor. The " spectacles " were mounted on the top of a stick with fore and aft movement, and they were rocked from side to side to give lateral control.

The spectacles formed a " natural " and easily learnt method of controlling an aeroplane, and it is not surprising that they are used in some of the newest and fastest aeroplanes of 1938. The pupil, as I said, placed his hands over the hands of his instructor when he began to learn, and usually this was after his total experience in the air consisted of a single circuit and landing. He noted with astonishment the movements made by the instructor in taking off, correcting for bumps and landing, and before the astonishment had even begun to give way to understanding, the instructor would require him to work the spectacles without assistance. Few things were more impressive than the movements made by the front elevator on its outriggers in response to fore and aft movements of the stick. If the pupil was not careful he became so fascinated by these movements that he forgot to note how the aeroplane was behaving. Then the instructor would take his hands off the spectacles and the pupil, still perched precariously above and behind, would seek to grapple with them. Again, long before he had begun to understand what was happening—in one instance, at any rate, it was forty minutes after the pupil's first flight—the pupil was told to go solo.

Now this is the tribute to the Maurice Farman : that it " mothered " these fantastic, ignorant, under-instructed pupils round the aerodrome and mothered them safely on to the ground again. The crashes were many. That is freely admitted, and it was inevitable when pupils were being rushed through their training so quickly ; but the extraordinary thing is that there were not more accidents and more deaths. The credit for that is due in large measure to the Maurice Farman Longhorn, the aeroplane with a heart, which took care of those who were supposed to be taking care of it. When a pupil made a bad landing and broke something in the undercarriage, the instructor would rush out and curse the wretched pupil. It was a pathetic sight to see one of those luckless pupils, goggling under his crash hat, white and wondering, under the shower of abuse from his instructor ; but the sentimentally-inclined would find the aspect of the bent and possibly battered Maurice Farman Longhorn still more pathetic. It seemed to feel that all the responsibility rested upon its frail shoulders and to be heart-broken for the lapse which had brought such fury upon the head of its pupil pilot.

At any rate, many of those who learnt under the stress of war in a Maurice Farman Longhorn can thank the aeroplane more than the instructors for coming through alive. The Longhorn was not only slow whether flying level at maximum speed, climbing or diving vertically, but it also formed around the crew a protective cage.   There were innumerable things in its 58 ft. 8 in. of span and 32 ft. of length to crumple and break the fall.   It was impossible for the pilot to go into anything " head first."   If he went towards his accident in a forward direction the front elevator and outriggers took the shock.   If he fell sideways there were corridors of wings, wire and wood to crash and crumple before he received the shock.

A mother among aeroplanes, a mother which yet, in her day, had been a reigning beauty and had broken records and taken part in races, the old Maurice Farman Longhorn has a firm place in the hearts of thousands of pilots of the pre-war and early war periods.

THE HENRI FARMAN

THE HENRI FARMAN

The Maurice Farman's lively sister was the Henri Farman. Delicate, elegant, quick, with fineness in every line and every movement, the Henri Farman in her early form possessed in high degree the mysterious quality of magnetism and to some extent she retained it when, later on, she became a pioneer of metal construction. She was like those lucky people one sees in the advertisements who are the centre of an admiring throng, while the poor old Maurice was more usually on the outside, looking gloomily on—an outcast, clumsy, self-conscious, unattractive. And if I am doing an unjustice to the Maurice by thus contrasting it with the Henri, I think that I make amends in the commentary on the Maurice. For ugly sisters have their uses.

My first recollection of the original Henri Farman, the one with Gnôme engine and big span top plane and small span bottom plane, was at Hendon before the war of 1914 when I saw Chevilliard doing vertical turns and his celebrated " chûtes de côté." To see that delicate and extraordinarily pretty top plane, with its scalloped trailing edge and its fine, almost transparent fabric covering, tip over into a vertical bank in those days was a sight indeed. Chevilliard was the right man to show off the Henri Farman, for he had the right sort of dash, but it always seemed curious that this most French of French aeroplanes should have been designed by a person who was English by birth.

The Henri did a tremendous amount of flying at Hendon before the War, and it took part in many of the races and exhibition flights. Later in 1914-15 it was used for training military pilots, and early gun trials were done in this machine. Early Service Henri Farmans had union jacks painted on the wings, a form of marking later superseded by the red, white and blue cockade. Some early Henri Farmans were fitted with floats and were used by the Royal Naval Air Service.

The Henri Farmans illustrated by Leonard Bridgman are the Gnôme-engined one and the all-steel Canton-Unné-engined one. The wood Henri Farman was designed in 1912. Late in 1914 Henri Farman was building in Paris the metal version which was made mainly of steel tubing. It was fitted with the 140 h.p.

Canton-Unné engine, a liquid-cooled radial, and it seemed suitable for tropical flying. Consequently an order for twelve was given by the Admiralty, delivery being promised in February, 1915.

There were delays in production ; perhaps I may be permitted to call them typical delays. The first was delivered in January, 1915, but only two more had been received by March. These first three Henri Farmans formed part of the equipment of the flying unit which left England on 15th March for service in German South-West Africa, where they acquitted themselves well.

" The War in the Air " reports that : " The Henri Farman aeroplanes came well out of the ordeal of flying in a hot atmosphere, their steel structure standing up to the climate where wood, no matter how well seasoned, must have warped badly. The only wood parts—the struts between the tail outriggers—did warp, and a number of men were employed almost continuously in making new struts. The Canton-Unné engines proved reliable, and there was only one instance of a forced landing caused by engine failure."

At the conclusion of the South-West African campaign in July, 1915, the South African air unit returned to England for further training and to form No. 26 (South African) Squadron, R.F.C. This squadron, in January, 1916, went to German East Africa and eight Henri Farmans followed in May to augment the original equipment of B.E2cs. Owing to faulty material the Henri Farmans had to be reconstructed before they could be trusted to fly over jungle country and there was only enough sound material for the complete reconstruction of three machines. These three bore the brunt of the long advance to the Rufiji and the Canton-Unné engines were once again, as in the South-West African campaign, to prove their reliability.

Four Henri Farmans were also dispatched to the Dardanelles where they were used for reconnaissance, bombing and fire-control work. Air Commodore Samson, in his book, " Fights and Flights," says : " We had a welcome addition to our strength by the arrival of two 130 h.p. Henri Farmans ; they were good weight-lifters, but unfortunately after about forty hours' flying, they began to lose performance owing to various weaknesses in construction. This was a pity, and we were terribly disappointed ; but later in the campaign I took the first 500-lb. bomb up in one." Later he says : " On the 18th (December) I took up a 500-lb. bomb on a Henri ; this was by far the biggest bomb that up to date had been dropped from an aeroplane in the War. The Henri took it up like a bird, much to my delight. I searched round for over half an hour between Anzac and Kilia Liman looking for a suitable target at which to drop it, but there seemed to be a lack

140 H.P. HENRI FARMAN WITH 500 LB. BOMB

that day of objectives worth while. Finally, I selected a long building from which smoke was appearing, deciding it must be full of Turks. I let go the bomb and turned round to see the result, but to my chagrin a cloud blotted out the ground. . . . It was only in 1919 that I saw the results. I had scored a direct hit ; the building, which was about 60 feet long, was absolutely wrecked, and amongst the ruins I saw no less than three bayonets sticking up between the bricks."

Two Henri Farmans belonging to the Royal Naval Air Service did useful work in spotting for the monitors *Severn* and *Mersey* in the destruction of the German cruiser *Königsberg* which had taken refuge in the Rufiji River. Good work was also done in the Mesopotamian campaign by all-steel Henris, and in addition to general duties their weight-carrying capacity was put to good use in the dropping of food and supplies to the beleaguered garrison of Kut-el-Amara.

The all-steel Henri was known in the Farman family as the F.27. It had a speed of 90 m.p.h. and could carry a load of 880 lb. Only the tail retained the characteristics of the earlier 80 h.p. Gnôme pusher. The F.27 used a Voisin type of four-wheeler under-carriage with band-brakes on the rear wheels. This undercarriage can be compared with that used in the earlier design in Leonard Bridgman's drawings. It had equal-span wings and the framework was all steel except for the tail boom struts.

This machine has a right to be regarded as one of the lesser-known heroes of the War, doing excellent work when well maintained by R.F.C. and R.N.A.S. mechanics, under difficult conditions in African and Eastern theatres of war. The early realization of the importance of metal construction is noteworthy, and credit must be given to Farman for his enterprise in making available to the British flying services a form of structure impervious to the ravages of tropical heat.

THE B.E.2

Born in one of the most stirring years of pre-War aviation, 1912, and the first British military aeroplane to land in France for the war of 1914, the B.E.2 and its immediate descendants were machines around which storms of controversy continually raged.

The name had its origin in the title "Blériot Experimental," or "Biplane Experimental," and the use of the initial letters set a fashion that has never entirely faded. Itself comfortable, quiet and competent, the B.E.2 provoked furious criticisms and extravagant praise. It was designed by Mr. Geoffrey de Havilland and may in some sense be regarded as the ancestor of the Moth. It started trouble during the military trials of 1912 when it assumed a lofty attitude of superiority on account of its having been built at the Royal Aircraft Factory, did not take part in the competition, yet went through the tests independently. The aloof attitude became especially maddening to those who had gone through the troubles and difficulties of the trials themselves, when it was stated that the B.E.2 had done a better all-round performance than any of them.

With the 70 h.p. Renault engine, a type which was later to provide the basis of the Cirrus engine for the Moth and which replaced the 60 h.p. Renault used in the early models, the B.E.2 had a top speed of 70 m.p.h. and a landing speed of 40 m.p.h. In that machine Mr. de Havilland wrote his signature, and if it is compared with the other D.H. types it will be seen that, although his hand has changed with the years, the signature is still easily recognizable. Look, for instance, at the D.H.9 or the D.H.5. The B.E.2 was designed to be automatically stable, a quality which was held by some pilots to bring with it many disadvantages when the aeroplane came to be used on active service.

Warping wing lateral control was used, and those who did not like it said that, in bad bumps, the pilot's knees were bruised black and blue by the violent movements of the stick. One thing that led to the B.E.2 becoming unpopular in some quarters was that, before the end of 1912, the famous ban on the flying of monoplanes by military pilots was issued by the Secretary of State for War. The conclusion to which the rivals of the B.E.2 immediately

14

THE B.E.2

jumped was that the Royal Aircraft Factory was being unfairly favoured in its competition with private aircraft manufacturers.

The B.E.2, however, went floating gently about the sky making friends and, to some extent, confounding enemies. Mr. de Havilland set up a height record of 10,560 ft. with it, and it showed a rate of climb from ground level of more than 360 feet per minute. The pilot sat behind his fencing of wooden struts and wires, with a good outlook everywhere except up and forward, with a four-bladed airscrew in front of him and with a whiff of hot oil coming back from one of the finest air-cooled engines of its time. This faint B.E. odour, if one may so term it, once smelt, was never forgotten. It came from the engine crankcase breathers which looked like elongated ship's ventilators. Their function was to " breathe " oil vapour from the crankcase on to the exposed valve-gear. They also breathed oil to some purpose into the pilot's face if he glanced round the windscreen. It was the exposed rocker gear, by the way, that led to one of the most excellent examples of journalistic inaccuracy. At this time the article on " My First Flight in an Aeroplane " was beginning its perennial popularity, and a woman journalist, taken for a flight in a B.E., wrote ecstatically of the " pistons dancing gaily up and down in the bright sunlight." Certainly if her pilot had noticed them he would have had heart failure. The aeroplane was adjudged " easy to land," and the impressive-looking skis which formed the front part of the under-carriage were highly regarded as a means of preventing the aero-plane tipping up on its nose.

Structurally the B.E.2 set the precedent which held throughout the Royal Flying Corps and Royal Naval Air Service period. The fuselage was formed by four longerons, with intermediate struts, box-braced with tie-rods. The rounded top part in front of and behind the pilot is fairing formed of light stringers, fabric covered. A spirit-level on the top longeron near the engine would give flying position for rigging the aeroplane. The top plane was formed of two wings and a centre section. Two main spars with compression struts and former ribs, cross-braced with wire, formed the framework of the wings. The undercarriage wheels had fabric covers to reduce drag.

The main planes were formed of two bays, braced with flying and landing wires and also with drag and anti-drag wires running at angles forward and aft. Apart from experiments, a straight-through axle was used for the undercarriage with shock-absorber rope to form the springing. The top plane had a small extension over the lower plane and its area was about 30 square feet greater. Controls were worked by cables running over pulleys, through tube fair-leads and to external king posts on the control surfaces.

Here, it will be seen, is the structural formula which ran almost without a break through the War and immediate post-War periods right up to the time when stressed-skin and geodetic forms of construction and the various kinds of single-spar wing began to achieve popularity. The aeroplane of those days resembled a Chinese nest of boxes. It was formed of a series of box-braced structures, the longerons, struts, spars and ribs being of ash and spruce, and the bracing of piano wire, cable and tie-rod. The turnbuckle was triumphant, and one of the rigger's chief occupations was the making of neat piano-wire loops and bringing the ends through the thimbles. Cable splicing was also to the fore, because the swaged, " streamline " wire, with its right and left threads, was not yet in general use.

Some B.E. detail features, however, were severely criticized. There was the unsupported rudder post, for instance, which was supposed to fold over in the air and was held to be the cause of several accidents. The B.E. went into production before the War at the works not only of the Royal Aircraft Factory, but also of Vickers, Hewlett and Blondeau, Handley Page, and British and Colonial.

The B.E.2 illustrated by Leonard Bridgman is No. 218, the one used by Captain C. A. H. Longcroft of No. 2 Squadron, Royal Flying Corps, when he flew non-stop for a distance of 650 miles. This was on the 22nd November, 1913, and although no claim for an official world or international class record seems to have been made, Captain Longcroft was awarded the Britannia Trophy for the feat. The machine was built under licence from the Royal Aircraft Factory by the British and Colonial Aeroplane Company, which was later to change its name to the Bristol Aeroplane Co., Ltd. In the front seat it had a special petrol tank carrying 50 gallons of fuel and the fuselage was streamlined over it. The route was from Montrose to Portsmouth, and back to Farnborough.

Previously, in a B.E.2, Captain Longcroft had flown 287 miles non-stop, carrying Colonel F. H. Sykes, the Commandant of the Military Wing, Royal Flying Corps. This was on the 19th August, 1913. The flight was part of a journey from Farnborough to Montrose, and the whole distance of 450 miles was completed in the flying time of 7 hours 40 minutes. Other feats were performed in 1913 by B.E.2 biplanes. They were represented at the King's Review on Laffan's Plain on the 3rd June, and also in the Aero Show of that year as part of the Government exhibit. On the 13th December, 1913, Captain J. M. Salmond, who was later to become Royal Air Force Chief of Staff, took up a B.E.2 with 70 h.p. Renault engine and climbed it to 13,140 feet, which was higher than the figure obtained by Mr. H. G. Hawker as a national record. Captain Salmond's flight could not be recognized as a national record, however, because of the aeroplane's French engine.

So important was the part played by the B.E.2 that a special interest attaches to individual performances, and two other machines must be mentioned—No. 206 and No. 50, the first belonging to the Royal Flying Corps and the second to the Royal Naval Air Service. No. 206 was the sixth B.E. built, and it had the 60 h.p. Renault engine. It was first used for experimenting with oleo undercarriages and was handed to the Military Wing in September, 1912. It was allotted to No. 2 Squadron, where it was flown by many of the early Royal Flying Corps officers. In February, 1913, it was transferred to No. 4 Squadron, and it was afterwards returned to the Royal Aircraft Factory where it was fitted with new wings and an ordinary skid and strut under-carriage. At the end of 1913 No. 206 had flown 111 hours 14 minutes or a distance of about 6,680 miles. Soon after the out-break of war it was overhauled by the Factory and fitted with a 70 h.p. Renault engine, and on the 18th December, 1914, it was dispatched overseas to No. 6 Squadron. It was the only machine to suffer in the gale of the 28th December, 1914, and it was sent to the Aircraft Park for repair and overhaul. It was returned to No. 6 Squadron on the 17th January, 1915. In the summer of 1915 it was fitted with a V-undercarriage of the type used on the B.E.2c, and in September of that year its career of three years ended with a crash.

B.E.2 No. 50 was delivered to Eastchurch in January, 1914. Commander Samson was among the officers who flew it, and it was he who took the controls for the Naval Review at Spithead in 1914 and for the flight to Belgium on the 27th August, 1914. Commander E. L. Gerrard, R.N., used it for the bombing raid on Dusseldorf in September, 1914, and Commander Samson used it for raids on Ostend and Zeebrugge on the 25th November, 1914. On the 27th February, 1915, it was flown home to England and shipped to the Dardanelles, where it was flown a great deal and where it co-operated with both the Army and the Navy in day and night raids, gun-spotting and other work. No. 50 was at work throughout the Dardanelles campaign, and it was not until No. 3 Naval Squadron was ordered home that No. 50 was written off and broken up as being unfit for further service.

The B.E.2 came into existence at a time when nearly all the best

c

aeroplanes were French. In 1913 it had a number of good British aeroplanes to compete with and, as has been noted, it was able still to hold a strong position. One bad accident occurred in 1913 with a B.E.2, but it may have been the result of inferior quality repair work. Neither the distance it had flown, nor the height it had attained was so great as the world's records recognized at the time by the Fédération Aéronautique Internationale ; but the B.E. had an easy-flying, almost a homely, quality which some of the higher-performing machines lacked.

Its homeliness was a distinct drawback in warfare, however. Indeed, its greatest weaknesses were discovered during war service, for the B.E.2 had not been designed for, or fitted with, gun-mountings. The B.E.2c, which succeeded the B.E.2, was armed in various ways. Sometimes the observer knelt or stood on his seat to use Lewis guns mounted on brackets linked by a bar between the rear pair of centre section struts. Sometimes a Lewis gun which could be fired downwards was fitted on the left side of the fuselage alongside the pilot's seat. Another mounting, which was found in numerous forms in the B.E., had one or two Lewis guns on splayed brackets which kept the bullets clear of the disc swept by the airscrew. But despite ingenious gun-mountings, the powers of manœuvre of the B.E. were unequal to the calls of aerial combat, and when the initial face-pulling period of aggression was past and air fighting developed, the B.E. showed itself totally unsuited to it. Launched amid controversy, it found itself during the War once again the centre of controversy.

But this at least may be said of the B.E., that it left its mark and its memory on the early days of the British flying service. It became part of the Royal Flying Corps of that time and through-out the War, even after it had disappeared from the active service squadrons, its influence was maintained.

THE B.E.2C

Most urgently and most frequently reviled of all war-time aeroplanes, the B.E.2c was an example of State manufacture which will always be quoted whenever the perennial problem of how far the State may be allowed to take over the production of armaments without impairing the efficiency of the fighting forces comes up for discussion.

There can be no question that several ingenious and highly skilled men worked upon the design of the B.E.2c, nor that it incorporated a large number of theoretically desirable features. On the other hand, there can be no question that it was responsible for extremely heavy casualties in the Royal Flying Corps. For, in combat, it was utterly incapable—the most defenceless thing in the sky.

Those squadrons that had to man the B.E.2cs did all they could to turn them to their purpose and to fit them with guns and gun-mountings which would enable some sort of reply to be made to enemy attacks, but for aerial combat the B.E.2c was fundamentally and permanently wrong. It could not be manœuvred quickly enough ; it had no effective gun positions ; observer and pilot were in the wrong places, and the Raf engine was never so good as the Renault.

So the picture which remains of the B.E.2c tends to be that of a small, spindle-shanked machine, with marked dihedral and " funnel " exhaust pipes, struggling to keep the air against superior forces. When low clouds limited the activities of the scouts and the bombers, B.E.2cs were over the lines doing artillery observation or other work. And every time they went out the B.E.2cs offered themselves as a target to anti-aircraft gunners and an objective to single-seater fighters.

Factory produced, the B.E.2c followed on in the traditions of the B.E.2, an early Factory aeroplane which is dealt with at length in another commentary. As flying machines, and not as war machines, the B.E.2cs with their large degree of automatic stability and their easy handling qualities were satisfactory enough. They could be stunted to a limited extent, and no machine ever went round a loop more automatically when once it had been set upon the right path, than a B.E.2c.

There were many accidents with this machine, but then, there

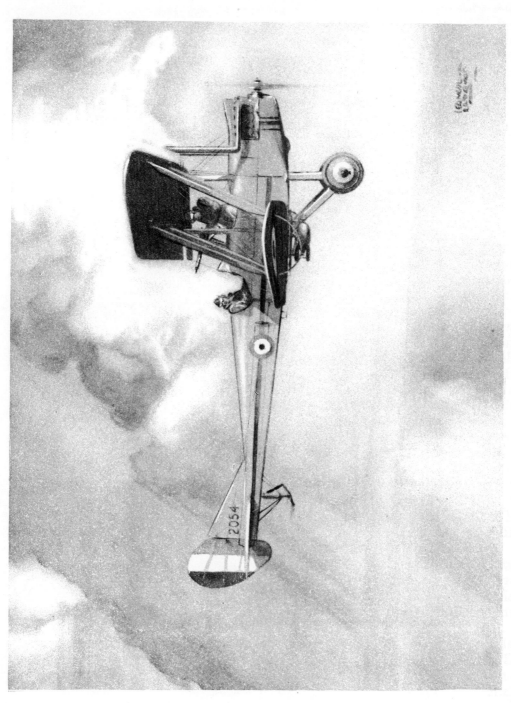

THE B.E.2C

were many machines, and it is difficult at this remove from the actual events to see how any particular or especial blame can be attached to the B.E.2c for flying accidents as apart from war casualties. But the B.E.2c will always carry with it the slur of having held back, because it was a State-produced machine, the progress that might otherwise have been made by the independent aircraft manufacturers.

It did not show any marked qualities of performance like the Sopwith Tabloid, for instance, yet it was used in large numbers. If machines were not chosen for their performance qualities nor for their fighting qualities, the independent manufacturer might well ask—as he did indeed ask—what were the criteria by which they must be judged.

Another thing about the B.E.2c is that it had a marked effect in influencing constructional and maintenance methods. The way in which control cables were to be arranged and attached, and the way in which rigging operations were to be effected and wires locked were all laid down in the B.E.2c, and other aircraft were made to follow that example.

In some ways all this may have been to the good, but in other ways it was certainly to the bad. It precluded just those innovations which might have accelerated aircraft progress. By laying down dogmatically what should be done it discouraged further thought upon the subject. Constructional methods in British aircraft showed the influence of the B.E.2c for many years after this aeroplane itself had been superseded.

The B.E.2c spanned 35 ft. and had a length and height of 27 ft. 9 in. and 11 ft. 4 in. Loaded it weighed 2,142 lb., and it could climb to 10,000 ft. in rather over three-quarters of an hour. This was its ceiling. The speed was about 72 m.p.h. Some B.E.2cs were modified by the Belgian Air Service and fitted with Hispano-Suiza engines. The pilot was then in the front cockpit. The performance of these machines was better than that of the Raf-engined ones, but not to any great extent.

So we sum up the B.E.2c as one of those characters in history whose influence was marked, but of questionable value when the well-being of the entire country is considered. Its name will be shadowed by the tragic months of 1917 when it was outclassed on the Western Front. It personified the State aeroplane versus the independently manufactured aeroplane. It may be unfair to put all the shortcomings of State manufacture on the shoulders of the B.E.2c, for there were many other Factory-produced machines, and some of them were good. But it has come about that the B.E.2c has achieved fame or notoriety—according to the way you look at it—as the supreme example of the State-produced machine.

THE B.E.2E

THE B.E.2E

A spidery-looking aeroplane, with lanky struts and spindly extensions, the B.E.2e was a development of the B.E.2c. It followed in the footsteps of the 2c and took up the artillery observation and bore the brunt of the attacks of the opposing fighters without having any really adequate means of defending itself. The pilot still sat behind and the observer some way in front of him, and there was usually no defensive armament for bringing fire to bear in a forward direction.

If attacked the B.E.2e had to try and manœuvre so as to give the observer a chance of firing at the opposing machine back and over the head of the pilot. The observer's gun-mounting took the form of a bracket or brackets linked by a bar mounted on or between the rear pair of centre-section struts.

One or a pair of Lewis guns were mounted in this way, and they were fired to the rear by the observer who stood up or kneeled on his seat. Sometimes a Lewis gun was mounted at the side of the fuselage on the left alongside the pilot's seat. This could be fired in a forward and downward direction only, and although it was adopted for a number of B.Es. it was not very satisfactory in combat.

As for performance, the B.E.2e was slightly better than the B.E.2c, and this was explained by the pilots of the Royal Flying Corps as being the outcome of the removal of the second wing bay and the use of the enormous extensions. But while those extensions were given the credit for improving performance by giving high aspect ratio and by enabling the second pair of interplane struts to be eliminated, they were also violently criticized on many grounds.

The wretched B.E.2e, which was really quite a pleasant flying machine as such, even though it may not have been well suited to war conditions, was said to " flap " its extensions, and many and marvellous were the stories which went round about what happened then. Some said that the aeroplane, if the extensions began flapping in real earnest, acquired a miraculous lifting power—like an ornithopter—and climbed in an altogether unheard-of way. Others said that the aeroplane at such moments became uncontrollable and fell to the ground.

Actually it is probable, though statistics on this point are nowhere available, that the accidents due to trouble with the extensions were few. The extensions looked weak, but actually they were braced with flying wires running out from the lower sockets of the interplane struts at a very favourable angle, and their only weakness lay in the landing bracing. This consisted of landing wires running out from cabanes arranged on the top of the upper plane over the interplane struts.

The angle of these landing wires was necessarily flat owing to the need to keep the height of the cabanes down as much as possible. Consequently the theory that if a B.E.2e were looped, and if, during the loop, it hung on its back, the extensions folded up, had a sort of basis in reality. But when the B.E.2e first came out—in 1916—when it was introduced for the Battle of the Somme, violent aerobatics were not contemplated as part of the war in the air—at any rate, by the Royal Aircraft Factory. Certainly a really heavy landing could cause the extensions to droop like the ears of a scolded puppy. That was probably as far as their weakness went.

The engine of the B.E.2e was the air-cooled V Raf, and the four-bladed airscrew—a factory fad—was fitted. There were also the vertical " chimneys " for the exhaust which were later standardized on the R.E.8. Fuselage, tail and undercarriage were the same as in the B.E.2c and so were the structural details.

The wing span was 40 ft. 6 in. the lower wing being 30 ft. 6 in. Loaded the B.E.2e weighed 2,100 lb., and its top speed was 82 m.p.h. The ceiling was about 17,000 ft.

Perhaps the most noteworthy thing about the B.E.2e was that it formed the obvious connecting link between the B.E.2c and the R.E.8. It is remarkable that these three types, in spite of the criticism which the earlier of them provoked, should have done the bulk of all the artillery observation work done by the Royal Flying Corps in France. And the R.E.8 shows almost as close a relationship to the B.E.2e as the B.E.2e does to the B.E.2c.

Pilot and passenger were changed round and brought close together, armament was brought up to date, wing loading was increased, gap reduced and the angle of incidence on the ground increased ; but on the R.E.8 there remains the mark of the B.E.2e. And as I have said, the B.E.2e, whatever its military shortcomings may have been, was a pleasant flying machine. In one of them I made quite a large number of forced landings in a short space of time while attempting a journey from Norwich to Farnborough, and each time I contrived, with but little skill and less experience, to get down in a field safely and, what was more surprising, to get out of it again afterwards and finally to deliver the aeroplane intact. That incident, perhaps, predisposes me in favour of the B.E.2e and makes me less prepared to listen to the adverse criticism that has been flung at it.

THE B.E.12

In response to the insistent call for performance and for a fighting aeroplane capable of fighting, the Royal Aircraft Factory produced the B.E.12 and the B.E.12a. In these machines, which may be called the first cousins to the B.E.2c and the B.E.2e, the load is put down and the power is put up. The only thing in which the B.E.12 failed to take the fighter further towards the type of machine desired by the pilots was in the armament. In fact, it may have been the shortcomings of the armament that had as much as anything to do with the failure of the B.E.12 to compete successfully with contemporary types of single-seater fighter produced independently by the British aircraft industry.

The form of gun-mounting on the B.E.12 was to have one or two Lewis guns mounted to clear the disc swept by the airscrew. There were brackets alongside the pilot, and the guns fixed to these brackets were splayed outwards. Control of the guns was either directly by hand or by means of Bowden cables. It will be seen that normal single-seater fighter tactics would have been impossible with these mountings. A B.E.12 could not be used for the circular chase combat because if the pilot succeeded in turning inside the other machine, he was still unable to shoot at it because he had no gun firing directly forwards. Pilots sought to overcome these difficulties by adopting a " crab " method of attack and by approaching their quarry on a transverse course. This involved complicated problems of deflection, and it is perhaps not surprising that the successes achieved by these means were not numerous.

Later, during the Battle of the Somme, the 140 h.p. Raf-engined B.E.12 was fitted with the Vickers interrupter gear, but even then the machine was of little use as a fighter, as by this time hostile machines made its clumsiness even more evident than it was at first. General Trenchard reported : " I realize fully that I shall lose two squadrons if I stop using the B.E.12 and delay, I suppose, for some considerable period two other squadrons. Although I am short of machines to do the work that is now necessary with the large number of Germans against us, I cannot do anything else but to recommend that no more be sent out to this country."

THE B.E.12

He went on to say that he would use the B.E.12s for the time being for night work, defensive patrols and bombing with escort. Later, the B.E.12 was used by certain Home Defence squadrons for anti-Zeppelin night patrols.

The B.E.12, therefore, and the B.E.12a missed being effective fighting aeroplanes more because of their ineffective armament arrangements than anything else. Had they been equipped from the first with a gun firing forwards in the line of flight by means of an interrupter gear, they might have competed with machines such as the Sopwith Pup and have led the way without intermission to the S.E.5. As I have pointed out elsewhere, the B.E.2c was followed by the B.E.2e and then by the R.E.8, all in a direct line of development. Had the B.E.12 been more successful there would have been another direct branch leading from the B.E.2c and the B.E.2e to the B.E.12 and the B.E.12a.

B.E.12s were used successfully for aerobatics, and with the 140 h.p. Raf engine—an air-cooled V, which followed directly in the line of the earlier Renault, which set the pace for such engines and was one of the finest air-cooled stationary engines produced—and the smaller Raf engine, the B.E.12 with its single occupant was capable of a fairly good performance in speed and climb, although it showed no exceptional height-holding properties like the Sopwith Pup. An objection which was taken by pilots to the B.E.12, although it is difficult to determine whether there were genuine grounds for it, was that it was too big a machine for a single-seater, and that, in consequence, its powers of manœuvre were too limited.

Whether that objection were true or not it is certain that in the early days of fighting in the air, the importance of high powers of manœuvre was very great and that no aeroplane could be regarded as a successful fighting machine unless it were capable of turning very quickly and of rolling from bank to bank in immediate response to the ailerons. The B.E.12, rightly or wrongly—and as I say, I am not in a position to judge the merits of the case—was held to be " too heavy " on the controls. This may have had something to do with its relatively short life as a fighting aeroplane ; but it is almost certain that the lack of effective armament arrangements had at least as much and probably more to do with it.

THE R.E. 8

THE R.E.8

A certain mystery attached and still attaches to some of the literal names which were given to aeroplanes emanating from the Royal Aircraft Factory at Farnborough. B.E. was held by some to stand for Blériot Experimental, and by others for Biplane Experimental, a difference of meaning which could hardly be more marked. S.E. was said to be Scouting Experimental and Single-seater Experimental, N.E. was said to be Night Experimental and Nacelle Experimental. But R.E. was Reconnaissance Experimental, and not the most ingenious quibbler could find an alternative.

The R.E. series, like the F.E. series, included a large number of widely differing types. The early R.E.5 resembled a blowzy old woman, and floundered about the sky in a safe if unattractive manner. The R.E.7, with 140 h.p. Raf engine, was another of the series, and then there was the astonishing R.E. three-seater with Rolls-Royce engine of 275 h.p.—a fearsome creation, with the front gunner standing up in the middle of the centre section with head and shoulders through a large hole. It was flown with a wheel control, and it went fairly fast for such an enormous thing.

This experimental R.E. was early in its career taken out to Candas, in France, so that General Trenchard, as he then was, could inspect it and obtain the opinions of pilots about it. The present writer had the pleasure of taking it there. On the way it behaved well except for a tendency to shed its exhaust pipes. A forced landing had to be negotiated on this account in France, but sufficient repair was possible on the field and the machine was finally taken on to Candas, where it arrived only a few minutes late.

Entirely different from the R.E.5 and this experimental three-seater, was the R.E.8. This machine was designed by the Royal Aircraft Factory to meet specifications put forward by the headquarters of the Royal Flying Corps in the autumn of 1915, for a standard Corps reconnaissance and artillery aeroplane to replace the B.E.2c. The R.E.8s were made under contract by a number of motor-car manufacturers and the Coventry Ordnance Works. With the F.E.2b the name of this aeroplane will for ever be associated with heavy anti-aircraft fire. No other aeroplanes, I

25

suppose, were subjected during their war service to such continuous and such heavy anti-aircraft fire as the F.E.2b and the R.E.8. In Leonard Bridgman's picture the R.E.8 of No. 15 Squadron is seen flying against a cloud background of exactly the kind the anti-aircraft gunners liked best.

The aeroplane is seen in a clear light without the dazzle of sun, and it is sharply silhouetted against the clouds. It is impossible to think of this aeroplane or to bring it to the mind's eye without expecting to see the bursts of high explosive and shrapnel shells about it ; the black and grey smoke puffs with the crimson centres, and the bumps and shocks of continuous " Archie " fire.

Army co-operation work was one of the chief tasks of the R.E.8. It went to France towards the end of 1916 as a replacement of the B.E.2e which, with its big extensions, may be said to have been a step towards it. The engine of the R.E.8 was the 150 h.p. Raf air-cooled V. Pilot and observer were very close together in order to give the highest possible degree of collaboration. For, in this machine, the pilot normally undertook the major part of the spotting while the observer's duty was to scan the sky and watch for enemy aeroplanes.

The R.E.8 was a single-bay machine with a marked extension and a strut connection between upper and lower ailerons. It was fitted with a four-bladed airscrew, and perhaps its outstanding characteristic so far as the look of the machine was concerned was the way in which the nose appeared to be cocked up when it was standing on the ground. This high angle of incidence on the ground was the outcome of a deliberate attempt to keep the landing run down. It was decided that this special step was needed to enable it to use small active service aerodromes in safety.

The big angle of incidence on the ground brought the wings in as air brakes as the machine stalled and touched down, and this did, in fact, help to shorten the landing run. But some pilots when first taking over the machine found a certain amount of difficulty in preventing the machine from " bucking " as it landed ; and some said that this tendency was the outcome of the big ground angle of incidence.

Other features of interest are the cowling and the exhaust system. The exhaust gases, instead of being expelled somewhere behind the cockpits, as in the S.E.5 and the Spad, from long exhaust pipes, and instead of being expelled from stub pipes or from a manifold as in the D.H.9, were carried up in two streamline " funnels " to over the top plane. The scheme was intended to give pilot and observer good working conditions and to prevent them from being incommoded by exhaust fumes. The tops of the funnels were cut on the bias so that the exit of the exhaust gases was aided by the slipstream.

The cowling included scoops which, to some extent, guided the air flow past the air-cooled cylinders and so anticipated the present form of air-cooled engine cowling in which the cooling air is controlled throughout its passage by scoops and baffles.

A shortage of supplies held up the production of this aeroplane at first, and later, weaknesses were revealed that had not been disclosed in the prototype. But although many troubles afflicted this aeroplane when it was first produced, in some ways it must be regarded as an interesting and a fairly advanced design. It did not foreshadow the future with any certainty—like the Bristol mono-plane, for instance—but it did show the directions in which designers were groping.

But it must be admitted that the lapse of years does not absolve from blame the authorities who decided upon the standardization of this aeroplane for artillery work. It was a bad choice. It was not a good flying machine, and its performance was meagre. The many accidents that occurred during the early part of its career were not always attributable solely to the fact that pilots were not careful enough. They were largely attributable to the fact that the R.E.8 was a less good flying machine than certain other types. The bad reputation of this aeroplane spread through the Service and following investigations and trials ordered by the Air Board, numerous modifications were made. The R.E.8 that emerged was almost a new type.

Some pilots will hold against the R.E.8 the fact that, if a bad landing tipped the machine on its nose, the engine was pushed back into the petrol tank and fire was almost a certainty. Riggers called the machine the " Riggers' Nightmare," since it had both lateral and longitudinal dihedral in the interest of automatic stability. But those who eventually got to know the R.E.8 also got to like it. Pilots would like any aeroplane if they were flying it long enough and were deprived of opportunities of flying other types and so obtaining standards of criticism. There is little doubt that, for its relatively low wing loading, the R.E.8 had a tendency to " fall out of the sky," and that this was a handicap to it through-out its career. It was not at its best in combat.

Really it was a compound of Aircraft Factory theories about stability. The marked dihedral angle on the wings was a Factory trade mark, to be seen in all the other types. The big extensions also fulfilled Factory ideas of the kind of cell which produced the best results and the high aspect ratio rudder and fin, the four-blader airscrew, the arrangement of pilot and observer, were all Factory schemes—some called them Factory fads.

At any rate this was the machine which was handed to our pilots, and this was the machine with which the majority of the artillery shoots were done. Those who were lucky enough to be flying in the individualistic (or non-Factory) fighters could look down with sympathy on those R.E.8s, going back and forth along their oval courses, through heavy anti-aircraft fire, and without much chance of success if they happened to be engaged by enemy fighters. The ceiling of the R.E.8 was below 14,000 ft., and at 6,500 ft. its maximum speed was 98 m.p.h. It reached 5,000 ft. in 11 minutes and 10,000 ft. in 39 minutes. Some score of squadrons were equipped with the R.E.8, and the machine achieved an enormous total of hours flown over the lines.

The standard armament consisted of a Vickers gun firing forwards through the field swept by the airscrew and a Lewis gun or a pair of Lewis guns on the Scarff rotatable observer's mounting, and it is interesting to note that the R.E.8 was the first two-seater produced by the Royal Aircraft Factory to have both these armaments. In a great many R.E.8s the forward firing gun was synchronized, so that the bullets did not hit the blades of the airscrew, by the Vickers gear, which was worked by bell-cranks and a long rod running back to the gun to trip the trigger. Squadrons sometimes provided their own armament modifications and some R.E.8s were equipped with individual gun arrangements.

Mention may perhaps be made here of the Prideaux link for the Vickers gun ammunition. This was a disintegrating metal link which held and formed the belt of ammunition fed to the gun. It got over the troubles which were inseparable from the Vickers webbing belt. In aircraft use this belt had many disadvantages. If it kinked in the chute after passing through the feed-block there was a stoppage caused by cross-feeding. There was also the problem of stowing in the restricted space available in a military aeroplane the lengths of empty belt. So the Prideaux link superseded the webbing belt not only in R.E.8 machines, but in all machines fitted with this type of gun.

So far as the gun sights were concerned the pilot used an Aldis tube (which was *not* a telescopic sight, although it is often so called) with a ring sight. The observer used the Norman vane sight, a most ingenious type of semi-automatic sight invented by Major Norman, who was killed after the War in an aircraft accident at Farnborough. The Norman vane sight consisted of an arrangement of small horizontal and vertical vanes mounted on a swivel which permitted tilting and lateral movement. The vanes were so designed as to area and position that, by the action of the slip-stream upon them, the bead was brought into the correct relation-ship with the gun's alignment to offset the gun-carrying aeroplane's speed and the direction of the gun.

The R.E.8 had a wing span of 42 ft. 8 in. for the top plane and of 32 ft. 7½ in. for the lower plane, so that the extensions amounted to over ten feet. The length of the machine was 27 ft. 10 in. and the height 10 ft. 10 in. Near the ground a maximum speed of slightly over 100 m.p.h. was obtainable. The weight empty was 1,803 lb. and loaded 2,678 lb.

Recollections of the R.E.8 are invariably mixed up with the pilots and observers who flew in them. For they were given an aeroplane which, even if all the adverse criticisms of it are dis-counted, was not as good as some; yet they made it work on a scale and with an efficiency as good as any. The R.E.8, often linked colloquially with the name of the noted comedian, Harry Tate, was one of the workers of the air war, and, outliving some of its bad reputation, it survived to the end as the standard Corps aeroplane. When the Armistice was signed there were fifteen R.E.8 squadrons in France. Continuously flying, continuously observing and, above all, continuously the objective of heavy anti-aircraft fire—that was the R.E.8.

THE F.E.2D

A cow, a blunderbuss, a domestic pet, a kitchen range with wings on, a threshing machine, a loutish, lumpish, heavy, clumsy old brute, a butt and a joke ; yet, among the aeroplanes of the War period, indubitably one of the great world's workers. That was the F.E.2b, forerunner of the F.E.2d and creator of the essentially big F.E. qualities. Look at this machine, and note the tiered nacelle, boldly opening its enormous mouth to gulp down as much drag as possible and then to ask for more. Look at the wires and struts, the undercarriage, the gun-mountings, and consider whether there has ever been or ever will be an aeroplane to express more openly and visibly its contempt for streamlining and all that goes with it.

In a squadron of F.E.2bs in which I served for a short time during the War, I obtained one impression which has remained with me ever since—that of a certain pilot of immense stature and girth, one of those enormous men who are yet well proportioned and do not look freakish but merely enormous, sitting upright in the pilot's cockpit of an F.E.2b on photographic patrol. There he sat, with Archie bursts all round him, an immense figure in a bright yellow leather coat, facing the rush of air, presenting his whole enormous frontal area to it, apparently impervious to the crash of shells about him, sitting up there in mid air, a monument of a man, an Epstein-like carving out of solid rock, miraculously supported on an exposed seat by a fantastic contraption. That pilot was the personification of the F.E.2b and of the F.E.2d, which was the same machine with a bigger engine.

I do not know what happened to him. When I had gone to a scout squadron we were occasionally called upon to escort the F.Es., and there he would be, again sitting in his exposed box with a Lewis gun beside him and the queer F.E. mounting and an observer squatting down in front. And all around would be Archie bursts and gun fire. He was one of the first, if not the first, to introduce the circular tactics which the F.Es. found so useful. When these machines began to be outclassed by the single-seater fighters of the enemy, they found that their opponents were able, by the use of their superior powers of manœuvre and their superior performance, to place themselves under the tails of the F.Es.,

THE F.E.2D

from where they could shoot at them in comfort without the F.E. being able to return the fire. It was essential for the F.Es. to devise a method of protecting their tails, and they did so by the roundabout method.

When they were seriously attacked they formed a ring and went round and round and round, each sitting on, and protecting, the next man's tail. In this roundabout formation the F.Es. were well-nigh invincible. In a forward direction they could bring a considerable amount of fire to bear, and in a rearward direction they were protected by the F.E. next behind. The only serious trouble with these roundabout tactics, was that they prevented the F.Es. from getting on with the photographic or reconnaissance work, and if the wind was in the wrong direction, the entire roundabout formation gradually drifted farther and farther over enemy territory.

A few words might be said here in praise of the F.E. observers. These were frequently seconded Army officers posted direct to squadrons from their regiments with no previous instruction in England. An observer was quite comfortable until enemy aircraft were engaged ; then he had to stand up, with only his feet and ankles below the gunwale of the cockpit, and work his guns while the aeroplane went through all the intricate manœuvres necessary in aerial combat. He had to hang on to his guns and their mountings to keep himself from falling out, for this was before the days of harness and there were no parachutes. Frequently an observer was saved from falling out, particularly when wounded, by the pilot grabbing him.

A Factory production, the original F.E.2b was fitted with the 120 h.p. Beardmore engine, and it may be mentioned that this engine suited it well in appearance, for it had the correct fire-engine aspect, with separate cylinders with copper water jackets. The machine at first had an exceedingly complicated tricycle undercarriage with a front wheel for preventing nosing over on the ground and with oleo operation of the shock-absorber legs. It was not the modern form of tricycle with the centre of gravity in front of the main wheels ; but merely an ordinary undercarriage with a third emergency wheel stuck out in front. But this undercarriage went through successive stages of simplification until, when the F.E. reached the end of the war, for it was used right up to the Armistice, the undercarriage was as simple as that of an S.E.5.

After the 120 h.p. Beardmore, the 160 h.p. Beardmore was fitted, but with this engine the machine was not at first successful. Cylinder holding-down bolts used to come adrift and, in the squadron which first received the 160 h.p. F.E.2bs, there were a good many forced landings through engine trouble, two of which were accomplished by the present writer. This was a great change, for the lower-powered Beardmore had a high reputation for trustworthiness. Its only fault was that it did not give enough power to cope with an F.E.

Finally the 250 h.p. Rolls-Royce engine was fitted, and it is recorded that the first of these engines fitted to an F.E. went straight to Germany. The pilot who was taking it out lost his way in thick weather. So Britain succeeded in presenting not only one of the first triplanes, but also one of the first Rolls-Royce engines to the Germans for their information and necessary action. With the Rolls-Royce the F.E. became a new machine. The engine bullied it and dragged it about in a peremptory manner, and made it do things which the older, more stately, F.Es. would have been horrified to contemplate. The speed went up to the dizzy height of 93 m.p.h. at 6,500 ft., and some of the more irreverent pilots who had been flying 120 h.p. F.E.2bs described the speed of the F.E.2d as " about double " that of their own machines. But it must be remarked that the 160 h.p. Beardmore F.E.2b remained in service after the Rolls-Royce-engined F.E.2d had been introduced. The F.E.2d was put on fighting duties and was then withdrawn, because the Rolls-Royce engines were wanted for other purposes, while the 160 h.p. machine was used for night bombing until the end of the War.

Here are the principal dimensions of the F.E.2d. The span was 47 ft. 10 in., the length 32 ft. 3 in., the height 12 ft. 8 in. and the chord 5 ft. 6 in. Empty, the aeroplane weighed 2,509 lb., and when loaded, 3,469 lb. At 6,500 ft. the speed, as already mentioned, was 93 m.p.h., and at 10,000 ft. it was 88 m.p.h. The climb to 10,000 ft. occupied 32·5 minutes, and the ceiling was 12,000 ft. Structurally the F.E. was of great interest. The curiously shaped, tiered nacelle was plywood-covered, and the front cockpit was of large size and gave the observer plenty of room to move about, although the edges were not high and, as previously mentioned, when things were happening he had to be ready to hold on. The wings were braced in three bays with pairs of interplane struts. The built-up, round section, wooden tail-booms were also cross-braced and strutted. The tail plane was on top of the tail booms and the fin on top of that, but the rudder came below them both.

The engine was mounted immediately behind the pilot's seat and the radiator, which was modified as to position in the course of development, and brought down and to the sides, was originally above and behind the pilot. It may be noted here that the F.E. took after the D.H.1, which was an aeroplane introduced in 1915 with a speed of about 78 m.p.h. and fitted with the 80 h.p. Renault engine. In general lines the F.E. followed closely the D.H.1 conception, but it was a much bigger aeroplane.

As might be expected from this pusher design with the two rather ample cockpits, the F.E.2b and F.E.2d gave ample scope for the ingenuity of armament officers and pilots and observers in the invention of gun-mountings, and some extremely interesting devices were used to give the machine the greatest possible field and volume of fire. The F.E.2b had a single Lewis gun fitted on a bracket attached to the front of the nacelle and operable by the observer ; but the F.E.2d had sometimes four guns, each on a separate mounting. One was in a similar position to that of the F.E.2b, giving the observer his forward field of fire, another was on a vertical mounting in front of the pilot's cockpit. This was also used by the observer for firing back over the top plane. Then there was a third Lewis on a Foster type of mounting on the centre section, which was used, mainly by the pilot, for firing back over the top plane, and finally there was a fixed pilot's gun mounted on the left of the nacelle and firing forward.

As might be expected, this wealth of armament gave rise to a wealth of different methods of using it. But it is of great interest to note that some of the most successful F.E.2d pilots constituted themselves chief gunner, and would go into action and manœuvre with the object mainly of using forward firing guns. Some of them mounted pairs of forward firing guns. And if anything in aerial warfare can be truly said to be comical, it was the spectacle of an F.E.2d blundering after some tiny highly manœuvrable single-seater and seeking to shoot it down with forward firing guns. It was as if the dignified old gentleman of the comic papers suddenly turned and went in pursuit of the rude street urchin. And as the street urchin would be astonished if the old gentleman showed a good turn of speed and caught him, so the single-seater fighter pilots must often have been surprised by the agility and pertinacity of the F.E. It must be remembered that the F.Es. were introduced when the first famous " Fokker Scourge " was rampant, and it was largely due to the F.E.s and D.H.2s that the Allies regained aerial superiority.

Although an enormous number of hours must have been spent by the F.Es. on photographic patrol, reconnaissance, fighting and acting as " bait " for single-seater fighters arranged higher up, they did a still greater number of hours night flying and night bombing. The F.E.2b was the standard night bombing aeroplane

D

of the Royal Flying Corps right up to the time when the Handley Page 0/400 appeared and set the twin-engine fashion. And after the 0/400 the F.Es. still went on, plodding over German territory night after night, performing their raids and returning and landing by paraffin flares. On some grounds the pusher design was criticized adversely as a night bombing aeroplane. It was said that it afforded no protection to pilot and observer in a bad landing. On other grounds it was advocated as giving the best possible view to the crew, and therefore aiding them not only during their operations over the lines, but also in landing and taking off. Certainly the F.Es. did a tremendous amount of successful night flying.

With regard to the duties of the F.Es. it is interesting to note that No. 20 Squadron, which arrived in France in January, 1916, and was equipped with F.Es. until the end of 1917, when it was issued with Bristol Fighters, is reputed to have destroyed a total of 600 enemy aircraft, which is said to be the highest total of enemy aircraft destroyed by any squadron in France.

One of the most remarkable experiments of the war was done at Orfordness in order to provide F.E. aeroplanes with protection against balloon barrages. One of these machines was equipped with a bowsprit, anchored underneath the front of the nacelle, and from this bowsprit lengths of stout wire were carried out and back to the wing-tips. Captain Roderick Hill volunteered to take up the F.E. carrying this protective device and to fly it into a balloon cable. And he did so ; the balloon cable was squarely struck, and it was deflected by the protective wiring and thrust aside, though not quite enough to prevent it biting into the wing tip. An electric spark was observed and the F.E. went into a spin. After a turn or so Hill righted it and landed. The protective device had proved to work ; but it knocked off a lot of speed and added a lot of weight, and it was never used in the squadrons ; so Hill's achievement did not bear fruit, and the fighting pilot again showed his preference for performance rather than gadgets.

Another F.E. achievement, which was done at Orfordness and is worthy of note, consisted in looping the aeroplane. It is hardly possible to imagine an aeroplane less suited to looping, but Captain Clive Collett (I spell his name from memory) held the view that a great many unexpected things could be done in the air if one really tried. He jumped out of an aeroplane with a parachute, for instance, at a time when this was a feat requiring great courage, a feat which few, if any, other pilots between Pégoud and Collett had attempted.

Collett did not wish to take up an observer for his attempts to loop the F.E., because he thought he might fall out of the machine. So in order to maintain a good flying trim, ballast was lashed in the front cockpit. Collett went up and, according to the reports of eye-witnesses, put the F.E. into an impressive dive during which the singing of the numerous wires rose to a shriek. Then Collett persuaded the old aeroplane up and over, tracing a figure which was certainly not a true circle or an ellipse, but, if the expression may be permitted, a circle with knobs on. On coming out he found that the ballast in front had been partly displaced, so he left the F.E. to fly by itself, undid his belt and climbed into the front cockpit. After securing the ballast he again looped the F.E. Whether this manœuvre was done by other F.E. pilots I do not know. None of those in the squadron in which I served attempted the manœuvre or knew of anyone who had.

There is one other F.E.2b incident which has little to do with the aeroplane itself, but which shows the conditions under which it worked. The F.E.2bs had been on a night bombing raid, and they went out and returned to their aerodrome one by one. As often happened, the illumination of the aerodrome paraffin flares, to allow the first machine to land, was followed by the falling of bombs on the aerodrome. A German aeroplane had seized the opportunity afforded by the flares to guide him to his objective. It happened that a large dog on the aerodrome was frightened by the bombing and began running wildly about, finally knocking over a flare and getting blazing paraffin on his coat. The result was that he ran faster until it went out, and the pilot of an F.E., circling to land, saw an additional flare spring into existence and go dashing about the aerodrome. In consequence of the uncertainty created by the moving flare as to wind direction, the pilot landed down wind and crashed. Fortunately for the story neither dog nor crew was seriously hurt.

Such was the F.E.2b and its more powerful relative, the F.E.2d. A real worker among aeroplanes—not, perhaps, handsome or fast, but a worker—a machine which could go on and on and did go on and on, tackling all kinds of different tasks and doing them all well.

THE F.E.8

Imitation is the sincerest form of flattery and the Royal Aircraft Factory hastened to flatter the D.H.2 when it produced the F.E.8. Between the D.H.2 and the F.E.8 there were slight differences in handling qualities and in performance, the F.E.8 showing an improved top speed with the same Monosoupape engine. But in essence they were two slightly different interpretations of the same idea which originated in the D.H. There was no new idea in the F.E.8.

Like the D.H.2 it was mainly built of wood, wires and fabric. It had the same general arrangement of wings and nacelle, but the nacelle had a rather more pointed nose, with a rather more marked down slope from the dash. The gun-mounting for the single Lewis gun was slightly different, and the controls were differently shaped for a reason which will be mentioned shortly. But the most marked structural difference was the tail-boom arrangement.

In the D.H.2, as will be seen if the drawing of this machine is looked at, the tail booms formed a triangle when seen in plan, whereas in the F.E.8 they formed a triangle when seen in side elevation. In other words, the tail booms of the D.H.2 were brought together on a vertical line at the stern post of the machine, whereas those of the F.E.8 were brought together at a horizontal line on the main spar of the tail plane.

Precisely why the Factory should have made this change is not clear. It may have been a change for the sake of a change and to avoid the possibility of its being said that the F.E.8 was a copy of the D.H.2. Both the D.H.2 and the F.E.8 represented a British attempt to adopt and improve on a foreign fighting method. Roland Garros had proposed a fixed gun firing forwards in the line of flight with a form of interrupter gear to prevent the bullets damaging the airscrew blades.

In other words the plan of Garros visualized arranging the aeroplane as a tractor and then introducing a device which would allow the gun to fire forwards in the line of flight. The gun was made to suit the aeroplane, but the British designers, with commendable ingenuity, decided to attempt to make the aeroplane suit the gun. Instead of thinking of modifying the gun fire so as

THE F.E.8

to fit in with a machine with an airscrew in front, they modified
the aeroplane so as to bring the airscrew behind and to avoid
putting anything in front of the gun.

The result was the pusher fighter. It descended from the D.H.1,
the Vickers " gun bus " and others, and became the D.H.2 and
the F.E.8. In the air the F.E.8 showed good performance
qualities for a pusher, but it is in that final qualification, " for a
pusher," that its downfall is to be found. Had the pusher been
able to compete and to keep on competing with the tractor in
performance, it is likely that the end of the War would have seen
pushers still in wide use for fighting purposes, and they might
even to-day be still in service in the Royal Air Force. But the
pusher could not keep pace in performance with the tractor and
the result was that, as the importance of performance began to be
realized, the pusher gradually faded away.

With a nose like those false noses sold at fairs the F.E.8 was a
satisfactory flying machine, though not so pleasant as the D.H.2.
Its controls were stiffer. One reason for this may have been that it
was the development of the Factory theory of the high aspect
ratio control surface. The ailerons of the F.E.8 were of very
high aspect ratio and they were certainly stiff, though whether, on
balance, they were really much more effective than the lower
aspect ratio ailerons of the D.H.2 is a matter of opinion.

The F.E.8 was reputed for a time to be dangerous in a spin.
Then someone at the Factory spun it deliberately and extricated
it—thus another rumour was killed. When approaching prior to
landing—which is the time when the torque effects of the
Monosoupape switch-controlled engine became most marked—the
F.E.8 showed perhaps less tendency to swing than the D.H.2, but
there was the same quick lurch of the wings as the engine came on
and off as the pilot used the thumb-switch.

THE MORANE PARASOL

Early days of the Royal Flying Corps in France were Morane days. Nos. 1 and 3 Squadrons were Morane squadrons, and the early War pilots who escaped the B.Es. achieved the distinction of becoming Morane pilots. It was a fine aeroplane, this French machine, with its extraordinarily light-looking structure and its shaped fuselage. Built to the designs of one of the earliest French constructors, the Morane Parasol was used largely for reconnaissance and was in service in 1915, 1916 and 1917, while the Morane Bullet was the first aeroplane to be used by the Allies with a fixed machine gun firing forwards in the line of flight through the airscrew.

In the course of the commentaries on the various types of aeroplanes used during the war, I have occasion to mention the attempts designers were constantly making to get the wings out of the way of the pilot's eyes. They tried almost every conceivable arrangement. They sat the pilot out in a nacelle in front of the wings and produced the pusher in many different forms; they sat him out in front of the wings, but behind the engine, and produced the backward-stagger tractor; they cut the wings up into three narrow strips and produced the triplane; they made them of different sizes so that the lower one was narrow while the top one came about at eye level and produced the sesquiplane; they even tried the quadruplane, as well as the monoplane in various forms. One of these was the parasol form, and theoretically a good argument can be made out in favour of this arrangement.

Apart from the fuselage, pilot and observer in a Morane Parasol had an entirely uninterrupted view of the ground. They also had an entirely uninterrupted view upwards and to the rear. Forwards and upwards their view was restricted, but only slightly, for the plane was not far above the level of their eyes, and it was cut away drastically at the centre section. Consequently the Morane Parasol was an ingenious and to a large extent a successful solution to the problem of providing uninterrupted outlook. With the 110 h.p. Le Rhône, it had a top speed of about 100 m.p.h. The Morane Bullet, however, like most monoplanes of its class, was restricted in outlook forwards and downwards.

THE MORANE PARASOL AND BULLET

Perhaps the most remarkable thing about the Morane Parasol was its handling qualities, and certainly this is the most difficult thing to describe after the lapse of many years. The balanced elevator and absence of fixed tail plane may have had something to do with it, but it is certainly true that this machine was sensitive, only sensitive in its own way. Pilots who got to know it could handle it easily and safely, but the fact remained that the " Morane pilot " of the first part of the War was a term having connotations similar to those of the " Camel pilot " of the latter part of the War. It meant that the pilot concerned was able to fly a machine which had a reputation for demanding high qualities of judgment and touch.

The Morane Bullet was one of those numerous machines which were not appreciated at their true worth. Descended directly from the Morane, which created a sensation at an early Aero Show by being offered to racing pilots, with a guaranteed speed of 75 m.p.h., the Morane monoplane was really the prototype of the Fokker monoplane which did so much execution among the Allied aeroplanes. Thus it was again that the countries which originated a type did not appreciate it, failed to concentrate upon it, and finally saw it copied and turned into a big success by their enemies.

Machine-gun interrupter gears went through two stages—mechanical and hydraulic—and the mechanical interrupters could be subdivided into the crude and less crude. The kind fitted to the Morane Bullet was crude. It consisted of hardened steel plates, set at an angle on the airscrew blades, immediately opposite the muzzle of the machine gun. The bullets which chanced to synchronize with the passage of the airscrew blade were deflected by these plates and the airscrew took no harm. The method was astonishingly crude and had many obvious disadvantages, but it did show the way to the form of fighting tactics which has been employed by single-seater fighters ever since. The gun used in the Morane Bullet was the St. Etienne, and this machine was included in the equipment of Nos. 1, 3 and 60 Squadrons. A few Morane biplanes were also included in the equipment of these squadrons and of No. 4 Squadron.

In the air the Morane Parasol proclaimed itself at a great distance and could not be mistaken for any other type ; but the Morane Bullet was exactly like the Fokker when seen at some angles and consequently there was a risk of failure of recognition. To overcome this risk official instructions were issued that the Morane Bullets were to have their airscrew spinners, engine cowling and other metal parts painted bright red. The spinner and cowling are worthy of note in the picture, because they are the obvious parents of what we now know as the N.A.C.A. cowling and of numerous other types of low-drag cowling. The theory upon which they were constructed was that of securing a sufficient flow of air round the engine to ensure correct cooling without causing more disturbance than necessary. The Bristol monoplane carried the low-drag cowling further on the way towards the present conceptions.

Finally, in dealing with the Morane, it is worth noting, as can also be noted in the wonderful Sopwith series of machines, the influence of air racing. Before the War, the Morane-Saulnier, which was produced by M. Morane after he had left Borel and joined Saulnier, was the supreme racing aeroplane. Hamel used it, and in various forms, sometimes with wings clipped to what seemed then to be below the safety limit, the Morane set up some high speeds. The Morane was seen frequently at the Hendon race meetings, and it was handled by many of the best British and French pilots. Brindejonc des Moulinais was a Morane-Saulnier pilot, and it was in a machine of this type that he suffered his experience at the hands of the Royal Aero Club in 1913.

He determined to fly his machine from Bremen to London to take part in the Hendon meeting. On the way he met a typical London fog and this forced him right down close to the ground. He came up the Thames and then found himself over Hyde Park, whence he took the Edgware Road to Hendon. It was a fine piece of piloting under extremely difficult conditions. As a result of it the Royal Aero Club cancelled his competitor's certificate for low flying. In addition, Brindejonc des Moulinais was summoned to appear at Bow Street to answer the first two summonses issued under the Aerial Navigation Acts, 1911 and 1913.

He was charged with having, as one having control of an aeroplane, failed to send notice to the Home Office stating the proposed landing place, the approximate time of arrival and his name and nationality prior to beginning a journey to the United Kingdom and, further, with navigating an aircraft coming from a place outside the United Kingdom over the County of London without having first landed in one of the officially prescribed areas. Brindejonc pleaded guilty. Fortunately the magistrate was human and delivered an address of welcome.

But the incident does show how the officious interpretation of the law so often exercised in this country earns for us a reputation for exhibiting ill-will to visitors from abroad. The first summons under the Aerial Navigation Act was issued to a distinguished French pilot. For a fine feat of flying—as conditions then were—

the Royal Aero Club took away his competitor's certificate. Fortunately other pilots and other people in the world of aviation did all they could to remove the bad impression created.

When Gustav Hamel disappeared in May, 1914, it was in a Morane monoplane. He left Villaconblay to go to Hendon, landed at Le Crotoy and Hardelot and was last seen over Boulogne. Reports that he had been seen in mid-Channel were of doubtful authenticity.

The Morane Parasol was a very different machine to fly and very different to look at from the Morane Bullet. Except for the M type of undercarriage struts, it bore few points of resemblance. Yet it proclaimed its parentage clearly enough to those who knew it, and those who flew much in the Moranes—the " Morane pilots "—always regretted the passing of this fine aeroplane and with it the kind of handling qualities which it possessed in such high degree.

THE MORANE BIPLANE

Least important of the three Morane aeroplanes used by the Royal Flying Corps was the biplane. It was included in the equipment of Nos. 1, 3, 4 and 60 Squadrons, but it was never used to the extent of the Parasol. Nor is it possible to describe the biplane as a feat of design on as high a level as the Parasol or the Bullet. It shows neatness of general layout and that lightness of build which was so essential at that time ; but in general conception it must be looked upon as comparatively ordinary. Again there are the famous M undercarriage struts and again the shaped fuselage, with light stringers supporting the fabric covering on a more or less circular section.

Wing shape, too, resembles that for the Bullet and for the Parasol, and is on the same general lines as that used in the Morane-Saulnier monoplanes which were seen at Hendon before the War. Something is said about these machines in the commentary on the Parasol, but here it may be mentioned that the Morane wing shape was for a long time regarded as supremely efficient.

The essential feature, to which almost magical qualities of lift were attributed, was the out-sloped wing tips. It was said that these out-sloped wing tips obtained the best results from the air which tended to be deflected slightly outwards from the centre line as it flowed past the wings. Probably the theory of the time was all wrong. Certainly to-day the point could be finally determined in a few hours. But before the War and during the early stages of the War the theory was one which could provide endless material for argument and discussion.

There is no doubt that the performance of the Morane aeroplanes with the 110 Le Rhône was good. It was not markedly ahead of its time, but it was in advance of a great many other machines of the same period. Whether the wing shape had anything to do with it may be open to question, but certainly the light form of construction, the neatness of the design and the ingenuity of the wing and fuselage arrangement, all contributed largely to the obtaining of good results.

In the biplane it is to be noted that the M-strut undercarriage arrangement is echoed in the centre section, and that the machine has a single bay with two pairs of interplane struts cross braced

THE MORANE BIPLANE

with the usual incidence wires. As in all French machines, cable and piano wire were used for bracing and for controls ; the cult of the streamline wire never imposed itself on the French designers as it did on the British. This was largely because there was no Royal Aircraft Factory to impose it, for the streamline wire was open to several objections.

If the rigging of aeroplanes had always remained perfect, and if the adjustment of the streamline wires had always been correct, no doubt some slight saving in drag might have been achieved. But rigging was not always perfect, adjustment was not always correct, and in the air streamline wires were apt to vibrate as the " singing " noises they made during a dive testified. Whether in actual service they saved any drag is open to doubt. Certainly they increased the risks of failure through enemy action, for if a bullet bit into one it would go, whereas a stranded cable would still hold. Their greatest advantage lay in the elimination of splicing which went with them. Wire cable splicing took time, and with the right and left threads of the streamline wire, rigging operations could be performed more quickly.

But the French designers stuck to their cables and their piano wires, and in so doing they probably had as much justification as the British authorities had in going over to the streamline wire. In the Morane biplane illustrated by Leonard Bridgman, the low-drag cowling which is mentioned in the commentary on the Parasol will be noticed, and it will be seen that the slit to admit the cooling air is as narrow as possible and that the cowling is complete round the Le Rhône engine save for the underside where the exhaust is ejected.

THE SOPWITH TABLOID

Father of all single-seater fighters, the Sopwith Tabloid will be remembered as an idea and an inspiration, and also as the first single-seater scout to be ordered in any quantity for the British Flying Services. In its day it showed performance figures which, considering the power used, must still be regarded with respect and admiration. And it must be confessed that, if proof were needed of the ultimate superiority of the individual effort as opposed to the official and communal effort in aircraft design, this machine supplied it.

Originally built in 1913 as a two-seater side-by-side aeroplane, it has been echoed and re-echoed ever since. Few machines of the 1913 period have left so strong an impress upon history. And its performance can be compared with that of the latest types of machine, power for power, load for load—for the seating was side-by-side. There was no concession to the small cross-section fuselage to which later designers of touring aeroplanes were forced.

With passenger and two and a half hours' fuel the top speed of the Sopwith Tabloid, with 80 h.p. Gnôme engine, was 92 m.p.h., and its low speed was 36·9 m.p.h. It climbed from ground level at the rate of 1,200 feet per minute. It would be invidious to pick out two-seater aeroplanes of 1923, or 1933, or even of 1937 and to compare them with this 1913 design; but those who wish to see just how far aerodynamics have progressed with the aid of the Air Ministry and the other large and costly organizations which have been set up since those early days, may find a reference to the performance figures of existing types instructive when they are compared with the performance figures of this type.

The Tabloid was built for that great pilot Harry Hawker. He was to take it out to Australia. The principal dimensions are a wing span of 25 ft. 6 in., a chord of 5 ft., a gap of 4 ft. 6 in., and an area of 230 sq. ft. Empty, the machine weighed 680 lb., and loaded it weighed 1,060 lb. Consequently, the wing loading was in the region of $4\frac{1}{2}$ lb. per square foot. Leonard Bridgman illustrates his impression of the Sopwith Tabloid when he first saw it arriving at Hendon one chilly December Saturday, in 1913. The pilot was Harry Hawker, who was reported to have come from Farnborough, where the machine had been under test by the Royal Aircraft Factory.

THE FIRST SOPWITH TABLOID

An impression of the " Father " of all Single-seat Scouts, Hendon, December, 1913

Developments of the Sopwith Tabloid were the Sopwith seaplane, which won the Schneider Trophy for Great Britain in 1914 and which, it is no exaggeration to say, founded the fortunes of the Sopwith company, and the Sopwith Baby seaplane. When people question the value of air racing, it is always as well to allude to that early success of the Sopwith Tabloid seaplane. It was flown in the contest by Mr. C. H. Pixton, and in doing honour to this remarkable machine the facts must be recalled.

The race was on the 20th April, 1914, and it was flown over twenty-eight laps of a quadrilateral course over the sea between Monaco and Cap Martin. Each lap was of ten kilometres, and the Cap Martin turn was a hairpin of some 165 degrees. The longest straight was, two and three-quarter miles. The Sopwith Tabloid had been converted to a float seaplane for the race, and the conversion was ingenious. The Sopwith company originally planned the machine as a single-float seaplane ; but when flotation tests were done on the Thames near Eel Pie Island, it was found that the machine was unstable on the water. Time was getting short, so the Sopwith company decided on a drastic measure.

The single float was taken off and sawn down the middle. The open sides were then boarded up and the single-float machine became a twin-float machine. Hurried tests were made on the Thames and were completed just in time to ship the machine to Monaco. Mr. T. O. M. Sopwith himself supervised the arrangements there. There were French, German and American entries.

Pixton, however, soon showed that in the Sopwith Tabloid there was a machine of which world aviation would have to take note. He went away at a speed of 88·9 m.p.h. for the first fifty kilometres, more than 23 m.p.h. faster than the next fastest machine, a French Nieuport. Pixton eventually crossed the finishing line having completed the course at an average of 85·5 m.p.h. After crossing the finishing line Pixton opened up his engine, which was the 100 h.p. Gnôme, and did two extra laps for speed record purposes. The little machine responded magnificently and the speed registered was 92 m.p.h.

That performance, by that hastily converted Sopwith Tabloid, was to have world-wide repercussions. For up till then Britain had been believed—not, perhaps, without justification—to be lamentably behind in aerial development. Pixton's performance came as a complete surprise to other countries. *Le Temps* spoke of Pixton's flight as particularly meritorious. It was noted in America.

Here are some further details of the Sopwith Tabloid in its original landplane form. The fuselage was of the normal braced type with a rounded fairing on top, and it tapered to a vertical knife edge at the tail ; but at the nose the shape of the engine cowling was made to bear a close resemblance to what we now call a " ducted " cooling system. The top and bottom parts were brought over and round the engine, entirely enclosing it save for two small " mouths " through which the cooling air was admitted. Being a rotary engine it was also necessary to leave the under part of the cowling open to permit the expulsion of the exhaust ; but otherwise this must be regarded as an extraordinarily shrewd cowling design which forestalled present-day engine-cooling theory by a great many years.

The tail plane was of a span of 9 ft., with rounded leading edge, the plane with the elevators forming a segment of a circle. The rudder was balanced and was 3 ft. 8 in. high and 3 ft. across. There was no fin. The undercarriage was a twin skid type with single axle and faired wheels. The machine was box braced and there were drift wires running from the undercarriage skids to the interplane struts. The cockpit was under the centre section.

The War Office ordered a small quantity of Tabloid landplanes as single-seater scouts. The only modification demanded was that ailerons should be fitted instead of warp control.

Royal Naval Air Service pilots used the Sopwith Tabloid to bomb the airship sheds at Cologne and Dusseldorf in October, 1914. The pilots on this occasion were Squadron Commander Spenser Grey and Flight Lieutenant R. L. G. Marix. The Sopwith Tabloid should always be remembered not only on account of its special merits as an aeroplane, but also because it provided one of the few genuine surprises which aviation has offered. This surprise was twofold. Firstly, the Tabloid surprised the British public by being an entirely British aeroplane (for hitherto they had thought that all good aeroplanes were foreign), and secondly, it surprised the entire world by winning the Schneider Trophy for Great Britain in 1914. When Harry Hawker, on the occasion here depicted by Leonard Bridgman, first came to Hendon with the machine and introduced it to the public, it created genuine astonishment by its speed. He made a couple of fast circuits of the aerodrome and amazed those who were there by the handling qualities and the evidence of speed.

THE SOPWITH PUP

The perfect flying machine. This is the term which the Sopwith triplane nearly fulfilled and which the Sopwith Pup did fulfil. As a military aircraft it had certain shortcomings, but as a flying machine—a machine which gave a high return in speed and climb for a given expenditure of horse-power, which had well-balanced, powerful controls, which was stable enough but not too stable, which was sensitive enough without being too sensitive, and which obeyed its pilot in a way that eventually secured his lasting admiration and affection—the Sopwith Pup was and still is without superior.

No statistics on the subject are available, but experience suggests that the Sopwith Pup was one of the safest aeroplanes ever produced. Its handling qualities were so good and its wing loading so light that it could be put down " anywhere " by a pilot who knew it well. And when once he was used to the rather powerful and quick elevator, the Pup presented no flying difficulties whatever to the novice. In the make-up of the Pup was the almost perfect engine—certainly the finest rotary engine ever made—the 80 h.p. Le Rhône. This was a sweet running entirely amiable engine capable of an excellent horse-power rendering and able to withstand harsh treatment when the occasion arose.

The present writer, when flying an 80 h.p. Le Rhône Sopwith Pup, was attacked by five German aeroplanes when he had been isolated from his patrol a long way over the lines. He was forced to abandon heroics and to run for the lines, turning every time he was attacked to bring answering fire to bear. On that occasion the 80 h.p. Le Rhône was frequently forced up by means of what are now given the grandiose title of " power dives," but which were then called " shoving the nose down," to fantastic revolutions per minute. But the engine did not falter or give up, and when the aeroplane reached home it was running just as well as when it set out. If I can return in some measure now the service given me by that 80 h.p. Le Rhône, it would be base ingratitude not to take the chance.

The performance of the Pup was remarkably good considering the engine power available. At 6,500 ft. the maximum speed was 106·5 m.p.h., and the climb to 10,000 ft. took just over 15

THE SOPWITH PUP

minutes. Fifteen thousand feet could be reached in 30 minutes. The span was 26 ft. 6 in., the length 19 ft. 4 in., the height 9 ft. 5 in. and the loaded weight 1,225 lb. The tank took 18 gallons of petrol. These were the official figures, but as with most other War types the squadrons often modified them by one means or another. Alterations were made to airscrews, to the rigging and to the undercarriage and a mile an hour or a hundred feet of climb more were squeezed out of the machine. Some Pups were flown by their pilots completely " stripped," without even a windscreen or an Aldis tube, the ring-sight alone being used, and with small tyres. This stripping and cleaning up of aeroplanes which went on in active service squadrons is almost the opposite to what goes on when a new aeroplane reaches the service in peace-time. In war everything possible was done to cast overboard everything that was not essential to the work to be done. In peace time the object sometimes seems to be to load up the aeroplane with as many accessories as possible " in case " they are needed.

The fighting pilot on active service, however, had one advantage over the peace-time supply officer. He could tell exactly what sort of performance he needed. In the Sopwith Pup the pilots found that their speed was not high enough to be a predominant factor in combat. But the way the Pup climbed from, say, 8,000 ft. upwards and the way it could cling to its height were proved to be of enormous value. The Pup could engage in circular chase tactics at 15,000 ft. and keep circling without losing height, a thing of which no contemporary German aeroplanes were capable. It was this power to hold height during a dog fight that made the Pup a useful aeroplane, and it was this quality that the pilots sought to amplify. By the selection of an appropriate type of airscrew and by lightening the machine as much as possible the height-holding powers were enhanced. And these were the powers that made the machine a formidable opponent to the Germans and that enabled it to defend itself successfully even against superior odds when flying high. When the D.H.5 came out it ought to have been better for high flying than the Pup according to theoretical reasoning. But in fact it was not so good.

When a large formation of aeroplanes was sent out on the Somme front it was originally arranged by the Wing Commander concerned that the F.E.2bs should be lowest, the D.H.2s next, the Pups next and the D.H.5s highest. But the Pup pilots were invariably able to hold height in the 12,000 ft. and upwards region better than the D.H.5 pilots, and when this was pointed out the layer arrangement was altered and the Pups arranged at the top with the D.H.5s lower down in the next layer. And this was found to be the best working arrangement, a proof of the Pup's excellent height-holding qualities.

The Sopwith Pup was originally ordered by the Royal Naval Air Service, and they took over some of these aeroplanes in May, 1916. By the end of the same year No. 54 Squadron of the Royal Flying Corps was fully equipped with them and was the first Pup squadron to go into action on the Western Front. A minor comedy of officialism was enacted with the Pup. Those in high places were grieved to observe this name " Pup " ; they regarded it as undignified, frivolous, slangy, unofficial and Heaven knows what else. So they found time, during the fury and trouble of war, to sit down and pen an order which called upon all officers and men to note that the Sopwith Pup was not the Sopwith Pup, but the Sopwith Scout Mark Something-or-Other, and it demanded that on all future occasions the aeroplane should be referred to under that title and none other. Everybody read the order and marvelled, and then referred to the machine as the Sopwith Pup. So another, more peremptory, order came out drawing the attention of all units to this prevalence of incorrect nomenclature. The aeroplane was in future always to be described as the Sopwith Scout Mark Something-or-Other. So I suppose that and the perverse state of mind of the fighting forces when it came to language, both good and bad, accounts for the fact that the aeroplane has ever after been known exclusively as the Sopwith Pup.

I have mentioned that No. 54 was the first R.F.C. squadron to go into service with the Pup. The Pup which is illustrated by Leonard Bridgman is one belonging to No. 46 Squadron, as the markings on the fuselage indicate. And these markings bring to mind another, lesser known, claim to remembrance of the Sopwith Pup, a claim which helps to put this exquisite little flying machine in its correct relationship to the rest of the development of war machines. The Pup was the last type of military aeroplane to carry individual as opposed to squadron and flight markings. And it was really the last type to be used as an individual fighting machine. Individual markings reached the supreme heights of ingenuity and elaboration in the Pup squadrons.

One squadron, which included among its pilots an artist of no small attainments, decorated its Pups with all manner of personal emblems and pictures. The majority had monograms containing the initials of their pilots painted on the centre section and fuselage as large as the area would allow. But in some cases pictures were painted which were supposed to denote the individual qualities of their pilots. An Australian Pup pilot, for instance, carried on top plane and fuselage a huge Kangaroo, beautifully executed in colour.

E

Another pilot, who was reputed to be a specialist in that kind of thing, bore into battle on the side of his Pup's fuselage what the Art critics would have called—with delicate euphemism—a " reclining nude." In the words of the squadron, it was a naked woman lying down in an attitude suggested by the pictures of Kirchner, the artist who created for many wartime men an ideal of voluptuous abandon. And it was very well done, in colour. Whether it created for its pilot any embarrassment when, in order to be presented with a decoration in the field, he was ordered to fly over to a certain aerodrome where troops were drawn up on parade is not recorded. Certainly Sir Henry Rawlinson, the General who gave the decoration, seemed both interested and amused.

Those individual markings took many forms and at the time they were of real value in aerial battle, for the technique of air fighting was only beginning to be developed and the outcome of any combat depended in large measure upon the individuals. Each pilot was helped by knowing who was fighting beside him, for the methods of each were determined not by rules but by individual characteristics. The wild man would be wild in combat, the stubborn man stubborn, the cunning man cunning. And each pilot, in those early battles, had to know and adjust his own procedure to that of those who were fighting with him. The fully decorated Pups of the kind I have been mentioning were picturesque, and some of the colour, in every sense, went out of air fighting when individual markings were prohibited and only squadron and flight markings allowed. But it was a logical development ; it was in parallel to air fighting changes. Air fighting had changed from the clash of individuals with individual methods to the clash of teams with team methods. It was appropriate that the markings should alter and that the team should be marked as a team.

So the Sopwith Pup stands out from all other war-time aeroplanes as the perfect flying machine and as the last of the individual air fighting machines. It is true, of course, that air fighting remained until the end of the war largely an affair of individuals. Single pilots still performed feats of note single-handed ; but there was a move towards formation fighting throughout the war and towards the end of the war, although the stage of co-ordinated manœuvre reached to-day was still far away, there had been much progress from the individual to the team. For the absolute individualist the Pup, at the outset of its career, was as good as any other aeroplane. It had the single Vickers gun, with mechanical interrupter gear, fired by a short horizontal lever or trigger which projected back from under the rear part of the gun and was pressed downwards by the pilot. In combat many remarkable achievements are to the credit of the Pup, but I shall confine myself to recording two accidents, both of a remarkable kind and both indicating the strong hold on life of this little machine.

The first accident occurred to Oliver Sutton, inventor of the Sutton shoulder-straps, as he himself called them, and the Sutton fighting harness as they have more recently been called. Sutton was in a Sopwith Pup squadron during the early part of this machine's fighting career. He was on patrol when the formation was engaged in a dog-fight with a number of Albatros V Strutters. Sutton was engaged with one machine which, after manœuvring, made a head-on attack. Sutton replied in the same way, the two aeroplanes flying straight towards one another, nose to nose, shooting. This is an unsatisfactory method of fighting, because both pilots seek to continue on their course as long as possible directly towards the other machine, each hoping that the other man will pull away first. Numerous collisions occurred as a result of these tactics and the tenacity of the two pilots. A collision occurred in this case.

Neither Sutton nor the German would pull out, and as the combined speed of the two aeroplanes after their approach dives must have been in the region of 250 to 300 m.p.h., there was little time for weighing up chances. Sutton decided that things had gone far enough, and he pulled out and up in a left-hand Immelmann turn. But he was a fraction of a second too late, and his top left wing tip caught the Albatros's upper right wing about midway between the fuselage and the interplane strut. The Albatros folded up and went down with a wing flapping. The Pup, although quite a large piece of the wing tip had been smashed up in a manner equivalent to cutting it off, still held the air, and Oliver Sutton contrived to get it back to his squadron's aerodrome. Two theories for the way the German had held to his course were advanced—that he had been shot through the head early in the encounter and was sitting there with the Albatros flying itself, and that the German pilot was deliberately trying to ram Sutton's machine. Both theories fit the fact that, at the beginning of the head-on rush, Sutton heard his opponent's machine gun, but did not hear it towards the end of the rush.

The other Pup accident also shows the way this little machine clung to life. A pilot was engaged in a combat when a strut of his machine was shot away and the lower wing folded up. The aeroplane went into a spin with collapsed wing at about 16,000 ft. and when the rest of the patrol returned they reported the facts and assumed that the pilot had been killed. One of them had seen the machine spinning for a long period. It was a long time afterwards that news came through that the pilot was alive and well. He had not been hit by his opponent's bullets in the fight and had been in full possession of his faculties when his Pup had been shot down with a broken wing. During the 16,000 ft. spin he had tried to climb out on the lower wing to force it down and so regain control, but he had not succeeded. So he had climbed back and wedged himself as well as he could in the cockpit in such a way that his body might have as good a chance as possible of surviving the shock. But I do not suppose that the pilot or anyone else imagined that an aeroplane could spin into the ground from 16,000 ft. and its occupant survive. Yet that is what happened. The pilot, whom I met again for the first time since he went into that extraordinary spin in 1917 at the Schneider Trophy race in 1931, survived. I do not know exactly what happened, but it is to be supposed that the machine fell into trees or soft ground. But the Pup's light wing loading was such that I doubt if the vertical speed in a spin was much more than 60 m.p.h., and with a folded wing it is possible that some sort of additional drag may have been set up which reduced it to an even lower figure.

Finally, I believe that if a Sopwith Pup with 80 h.p. Le Rhône engine were to be introduced to-day, and if it were tried against the latest and best private owner types of light aeroplane, it would show itself to be—considered purely as a flying machine—at least equal to the best of them. Last of all, let it not be forgotten that the Sopwith Pup bears more than a family resemblance to the Sopwith Tabloid whose remarkable story is told in another of these commentaries.

THE SOPWITH CAMEL

Gifted with a more strongly developed personality than perhaps any other aeroplane, the Sopwith Camel inspired the pilots who flew it with respect and with affection. Once a Camel pilot, always a Camel pilot. And the very term " Camel pilot " held a special meaning and was in itself regarded as a sort of commendation. For this machine was known to be at once difficult and yet responsive ; wilful yet, with those who knew how to handle it, enthusiastically obedient. The Camel set a new standard in powers of manœuvre, and even to-day it probably remains the most highly manœuvrable aeroplane that has ever been built.

Two features of the Camel immediately impressed themselves on the eye of the beholder—the way in which the fuselage seemed to grow in a sort of crescendo effect from back to front, and to culminate in the hump or, more correctly, the hunched shoulders just below the centre section ; and the arrangement of the planes with the marked dihedral angle on the bottom plane and the straight top plane. So sharply did these two features differentiate the Camel from all other types that it could be recognized at great distances.

Most of the stories which centre on the Camel have to do with its terrific powers of manœuvre. It was the chosen instrument of the greatest aerobatic pilots, and the reason became plain in a few seconds' flying, for it responded to a touch. It could be " thought " round turns. From level flight it could be stood up on end so suddenly, by a mere easing of pressure on the control stick, that it would stall. That was partly why inexperienced pilots and pilots new to the Camel found difficulty in looping it. They failed to appreciate the great powers of the elevator, and used it too coarsely, with the result that the machine would stall on the up grade and fall out sideways.

But this very super-sensitiveness was an advantage to those who knew how to make the best use of it. It enabled loops to be made from a relatively low speed with the aeroplane under full control all the way round. It also enabled flick rolls to be performed without loss of height, and it gave the machine good powers of manœuvre when it was being flown upside down. When the aeroplane first appeared a rumour went round the Royal

THE SOPWITH CAMEL

Flying Corps that it was " stable " on its back and that, when once there, it could not be extricated.

This was the outcome of a crash in which the Camel, after turning on its back, dived into the ground while still upside down and killed its pilot. There were other crashes somewhat resembling this one. There were also crashes in which Camels spun into the ground. Rumour and counter-rumour travelled round the Royal Flying Corps and Royal Naval Air Service messes about these crashes, and all kinds of vices were attributed to the aeroplane.

But it seems likely that the theory finally put forward by Oliver Sutton was the correct one—that many of the upside-down Camel crashes had been due to the suddenness of the machine's responses throwing the pilot out of his seat and to his inability to get back in time. A slight touch forward on the stick did tend to hurl the pilot bodily out of his seat, and when Camels were first put into service they had only the safety belts and not the fighting harness.

The importance of holding the pilot down firmly on his seat was not appreciated when the Camel was first introduced, because other machines had had so much slower responses, and because upside-down flying was still uncommon in the services. But with the introduction of the Camel and with the growth of familiarity with its habits, upside-down flying became commoner and with it the need for shoulder-straps began to be appreciated.

It was Oliver Sutton, already mentioned, who invented the first shoulder-straps and who established the system upon which all subsequent shoulder-straps have been made. He has received no official credit for that invention, and even the name of the straps, which were first known as the Sutton harness, has been changed so that no link remains between the inventor and his invention. Sutton made not a penny out of the invention, and it seems that the authorities might at least have allowed his name to be associated with the straps.

The essential points about the Sutton harness are that separate pairs of straps are used for the shoulders and for the thighs, and that the methods of adjustment and quick release are co-ordinated. This quick release was the subject of a considerable amount of research by Sutton, for the problem is much more complicated than would at first sight appear. The essentials are that the fastening shall hold under all conditions and that there shall be no risk of accidental release, but that, no matter whether the pilot's weight is on the straps or not, the release shall act easily and quickly when it is wanted.

Sutton hit upon the plan of introducing in each of the four

straps a series of holes with eyes placed close to each other. He then used, independently, a conical pin of large diameter, with a small hole through it near the apex. The pilot, when putting on the harness, drew the thigh straps over tightly and looped them over the conical pin at the hole which suited his own particular size. Then the shoulder-straps were similarly looped over the pin, making four straps, one on top of the other, over the pin. Finally a spring clip was passed through the hole in the top of the conical pin.

The spring clip prevented the straps from sliding off the pin, but it did not take the main load. The pin was cone-shaped in order that the straps should tend to slide off. If it had been parallel sided they might have jammed on. With the Sutton harness there was no possibility of accidental release, yet there was no possibility of jamming, and the adjustment for the individual pilot was simplicity itself and was done at the actual time of putting on the harness. It was a fine achievement in the devising of a satisfactory aeronautical accessory.

The Camel brought the Sutton harness into general use, although the idea had been evolved before it appeared in the squadrons. The present writer had an opportunity on two occasions to test the harness in action. On both these occasions the Camel he was flying turned over on the ground ; once as a result of a forced landing on unsuitable ground, and the other time as a result of landing on an aerodrome at the instant a line squall struck it. The terrific wind turned the aeroplane over before the ground crew could seize it. On both occasions the Sutton harness held the pilot so that he was uninjured and not thrown out while the machine turned over, and he was able instantly to release himself by withdrawing the spring clip, the harness being immediately freed.

The combination of the Camel and the Sutton harness gave those aerobatically inclined their greatest opportunity, and they took it well. Looping was brought down to ground level, although then as now it was freely admitted that it was dangerous and foolish to stunt near the ground. Flick rolling was also brought down to shed-roof height. Captain Armstrong, an almost legendary figure, was perhaps the supreme exponent of low aerobatics. He was stationed with a night flying squadron at an aerodrome east of London, and here he frequently gave exhibitions of aerobatics which were perhaps the most remarkable ever done.

He specialized in loops done from a relatively low speed from ground level. It seemed that there was no possibility of escaping from a crash if the engine failed or faltered, although Armstrong himself always held that he had means of side-slipping out safely.

His flick rolls were started at less than the height of the sheds, and it is recorded that on one occasion a wing tip brushed the grass as the aeroplane went round. It will be noted that a flick roll is a far more dangerous manœuvre to perform close to the ground than a slow roll, because in the middle of a flick roll the aeroplane is auto-rotating. It is, in fact, in a horizontal spin and consequently the pilot abandons control for a moment, to regain it as the full turn is completed.

Armstrong succeeded in doing these flick rolls without losing height by starting them at about 80 m.p.h. and bringing the engine in fully as the machine went over. There was just enough thrust to hold the machine up as it came out in a stalled condition and at a big angle of incidence. Numerous other pilots specialized in aerobatics with the Camel, and for a long time the machine held an undisputed lead on its powers of manœuvre.

It was probably this that enabled the Camel to do so much pioneer work. It was used for deck flying, for night flying and for experiments of various kinds, including an experiment in " upward shooting," in which a gun or a pair of guns was fixed pointing upwards in such a way that the Camel could fly underneath a raiding bombing aeroplane and, provided the pilot adjusted his speed to that of the bomber, great accuracy of shooting could be secured at long range. Flags were towed for this work and some good results were secured, but the method was never extensively adopted for defence purposes. It might be mentioned here that, during the War, Camels in service with the Royal Flying Corps and the Royal Naval Air Service destroyed 1,281 enemy aircraft.

For ship use the Camel had only one Vickers gun, but for use with the Royal Flying Corps it had two Vickers guns firing forward through the field swept by the airscrew and " interrupted " by the Constantinesco hydraulic gear. The guns were mounted on top of the fuselage immediately in front of the pilot, and between them was mounted a ring sight and usually an Aldis tube sight, a form of sight often referred to, though not with strict accuracy, as a " telescopic " sight. The ship's Camel had a Lewis gun mounted on the centre section in addition to the Vickers gun. The rear part of its fuselage was detachable behind the cockpit for easy stowage on board ship.

The Camel engines were the 110 h.p. Le Rhône, the 130 h.p. Clergêt, the 150 h.p. B.R.1 and the 250 h.p. B.R.2. Other engines were also tried, including the 150 h.p. Monosoupape Gnôme. This was a remarkable engine, a development of the smaller Monosoupape, but with an unusual method of control. Instead of controlling the engine by means of a thumb-switch on the stick, by " blipping," it had a multi-position switch on the dash. This would cut out alternate cylinders by switching them off and leave the remaining cylinders in operation. The sound of the engine when it was being controlled in this way was curious to say the least of it, and it could be made to resemble the sound of a single-cylinder motor-bicycle or a continuous roar like the 100 h.p. Monosoupape, only twice as loud.

With the 150 h.p. Monosoupape the Camel showed its highest performance, but it never went into service with this engine. Another non-standard Camel was the two-seater, made for instruction purposes. The top speed with 110 h.p. Le Rhône engine was 120 m.p.h. and with the 130 h.p. Clergêt it was a fraction higher.

Outlook from the Camel was good, with the lower plane so far back relative to the pilot's position that he was able to look down at a fairly steep angle in front. The top plane blanked out a fairly large arc ; but in a great many Camels it was cut away at the centre section which gave a small " window " for looking upwards and forwards. The aeroplane was comfortable to fly considering its rapidity of manœuvre, and it had the celebrated Sopwith " spade grip " control stick with the engine switch in the centre of the cross-bar at the top and with the two gun triggers in the opening.

The Camel shown by Leonard Bridgman wears the three streamers of the formation leader. Camels did an enormous amount of formation fighting, and this machine must be regarded as the type which played a big part in the development of this form of fighting. It was a great machine, a machine which enabled pilots to discover the possibilities of aerobatics better than any of its predecessors and which also enabled a great many special experiments to be done which could not have been done had there been no machine of such marked powers of manœuvre.

It is no use denying that it suffered the faults of its good qualities. With its rotary engine and short fuselage it was subjected to the effects of torque, and it turned to the right in a manner entirely different from the way in which it turned to the left. Its elevator was criticized as being over-sensitive, and its ailerons as being too " stiff." But as a whole it provided a wonderful instrument.

It was robust and enormously quick and, as I have said, it evoked the admiration and affection of all who flew it. In consequence it is not surprising that, in addition to its normal war work, the Camel was used for much special pioneer work. There were the early experiments, for instance, with the Camel towed on a lighter behind a destroyer. These lighter experiments were conducted, not as deck-flying tests, but to evolve a scheme whereby a lightly-loaded, fast-climbing fighter could be put up at short notice anywhere in the North Sea to combat the high-flying Zeppelin scouts. The improved performance of the Zeppelin and its remarkable ability to climb and remain at great heights, defeated the heavily-loaded seaplanes and flying-boats which, operating far away from their shore bases, could not sacrifice everything else for performance. The first time the lighter-carried Camel was used in practice Lieutenant Stuart Culley shot down L.53 at 19,000 feet, exactly one hour after he took off from the lighter towed by H.M.S. *Redoubt*. The *Redoubt* was accompanying the Harwich Light Cruiser Force in some special operations in the Heligoland Bight in August, 1918.

Another notable flight was made in the summer of 1918 in connection with experiments initiated with a view to discovering means of providing aerial escort for our airships. A Camel, piloted by Lieutenant R. E. Keys, was dropped from the airship R.33, the pilot started his engine and landed at Pulham. Then there were the dive bombing experiments made in 1917 at Orfordness by the present writer. Dive bombing is often thought of as a post-war development, but actually the statistics upon which the method is based were obtained with a Camel in 1917.

The Camel can be summed up as a fine aeroplane which inspired everyone who knew it with real—sometimes fanatic—affection.

THE SOPWITH TRIPLANE

One of the select band of aeroplanes which gave their pilots pleasure because of their lightness of touch and their sympathetic handling qualities was the Sopwith Triplane, with Clergêt rotary engine, first of 110 h.p. and later of 130 h.p. The later Sopwith Triplane, the Snark, with radial engine, although it possessed a better performance and was a satisfying aeroplane to fly, did not achieve the supreme handling excellence of the earlier model. Indeed, the triplane illustrated by Leonard Bridgman and used largely by the Royal Naval Air Service must be placed in history as approaching closely to the pilot's ideal flying machine, almost equal to the Sopwith Pup.

Produced in 1916, ordered by the Royal Flying Corps, " swopped " by them for Spads, and introduced to the Royal Naval Air Service in the summer of 1916, at first the triplane was rumoured to be weak and it was stated that the wings folded up in the air if it were dived at all steeply. It was also reported to be subject to the same trouble as the Nieuport and to have a habit of twisting one of its planes about the front spar so that control and stability were lost. But in fact none of these faults was demonstrated to be inherent in the aeroplane, and as pilots got to know it better they came to like it better until, when it was superseded, it was allowed to go with regret. And when, in the Royal Air Force Display of 1936, a Sopwith Triplane appeared and flew, it still showed its qualities of fineness and delicacy and was as obviously a thoroughbred as the aeroplanes built in 1936.

It would be difficult to analyse the feature in this machine that made it so attractive to fly. It seemed light and elegant yet wiry. And there was the visual effect of the triplane arrangement which made the pilot feel that he had unlimited quantities of lift available. The response to the controls was not of that lightning quickness exemplified by the Sopwith Camel, but it was by no means sluggish. At first it was thought that the triplane could not be looped and flick-rolled with safety, but later it was made to do all the aerobatics of its time, and it did them well.

Captain Vernon Brown was an exponent of aerobatics with the Sopwith Triplane, and he successfully demonstrated that the aeroplane was capable of the whole gamut of aerobatics, and that

THE SOPWITH TRIPLANE

although it did not appear to do the manœuvres with the suddenness of the biplanes, it did them with infinite grace. The triplane spun rather slowly, and its flick roll was also rather slow compared with other machines of the time ; but what it lacked in quickness it made up in the smoothness and grace of its movements. A triplane looping looked like no other machine and gave the loops an individual quality. Irreverent pilots said it looked, when doing aerobatics, like an intoxicated flight of stairs.

So far as war service was concerned, the triplane was successful. It was used by many of the leading Royal Naval Air Service fighting pilots, and when it first appeared on the Western Front it achieved some notable successes. Indeed, there is evidence that the introduction of the triplane form had a psychological effect on the enemy pilots and made them believe that the capabilities of the aeroplane were, perhaps, rather greater than they were in fact.

With the higher-powered engine the triplane did about 107 m.p.h. at 10,000 ft., and its absolute maximum was 114 m.p.h. Its ceiling was 20,500 ft. and it climbed to 10,000 ft. in 11·8 minutes. The all-up weight was 1,543 lb. and the wing span 26 ft. 6 in. The length was 18 ft. 10 in., the chord only 3 ft. 3 in. and the height 10 ft. 6 in. There were the single, very wide, interplane struts and the flying wires ran up steeply from the underside of the fuselage to the top socket of the interplane strut. Ailerons were on all six wings.

In 1917 Nos. 1, 8, 9 and 10 Naval Squadrons were equipped with this machine, and a formation of triplanes seen from the air had a look like no other formation. The armament was one Vickers gun synchronized to fire through the field swept by the airscrew. One rather undesirable distinction was won by the Sopwith Triplane when it first came out ; for the first two machines of the type to be sent to France were landed, through a navigational mistake, in German territory.

Finally the evidence given by this design of that strong originality which marked the war-time aeroplanes must be noted. At a time when the biplane seemed to hold undisputed sway, it was possible for a designer to strike out with this entirely unorthodox design and, without offering any astonishing superiority over biplane types in performance, to get the aeroplane adopted for use in the Service. The remark is often made that, during the War, almost every possible variation of the aeroplane was tried ; and it is certainly true that the triplane form was thoroughly tried and its merits and shortcomings established.

THE SOPWITH BABY

Directly descended from the Sopwith Tabloid, and immediately related to the machine which won the Schneider Trophy for Great Britain in 1914, the Sopwith Baby went into service with the Royal Naval Air Service in 1915 and continued in service until the end of the War. Engines were changed and minor modifications to the airframe were made, but in essentials the machine remained the same, a noteworthy testimony to the lasting qualities of a good design.

The original Schneiders were built by the Sopwith Company and were fitted with 100 h.p. Monosoupape Gnôme engines. A later edition had the 110 h.p. Clergêt. An attempt to use the machine as a bomber, with two 65 lb. bombs, led to overloading, and consequent unpopularity, and production was stopped for further experiment and possible replacement. Shortage of seaplanes and lack of a suitable successor to the Schneider led to its revival with the 130 h.p. Clergêt. The Sopwith Company being at that time full up with other orders, the task of modifying the machine for the larger engine and preparation of new drawings for sub-contracting was entrusted to the Blackburn Company. The machine was sometimes known as the Blackburn Baby, although the old name, " Sopwith " was generally used by those who had followed its development.

As the power of the engine was pushed up so was the weight of the load, and towards the end of the War these little machines which originated as two-seater side-by-side touring aeroplanes, were carrying two guns, bombs, carrier-pigeons and sea gear.

The Schneider seaplane played an important part in the development of deck-flying. The early difficulties of seaplane carriers—having to stop to hoist seaplanes out of the water and the difficulty of seaplanes operating from the open sea—prompted the Commander-in-Chief, Sir John Jellicoe, to propose that the only method of combating naval Zeppelins was the use of aeroplanes rising from the deck of the *Campania*, the first carrier equipped with a flying-off deck. Within a week of making this proposal to the Admiralty a Schneider, piloted by Flight Lieutenant W. L. Welsh was flown off the deck of the *Campania*, when the carrier was steaming at seventeen knots into the wind. Wheels, fitted

THE SOPWITH BABY

under the floats, were dropped into the sea as soon as the machine was air-borne. The marks of the wheels along the deck showed that the seaplane had run 113 feet before taking off. This was in August, 1915. It was thus proved that small aircraft, whether landplanes or seaplanes, capable of attacking reconnoitring Zeppelins could be got away without exposing the carrier to the submarine danger which stopping to hoist out entailed.

It will be noted that the Sopwith Baby was a three-point float seaplane, the centre of gravity being so positioned that the tail float came into use on alighting. The cumbersomeness of floats militated against the use of this aeroplane for fighting, and gradually the landplane replaced the seaplane for oversea fighting and fleet use, and the Sopwith Baby was relegated to police duties such as are described below by a Yarmouth pilot. Nevertheless, this machine was used in many theatres of war—home waters, the Belgian coast, the Dardanelles, the Balkans, the Middle East generally and the Adriatic.

Its duties on the East Coast are best described by one of the pilots, who says : " The machine was naturally a little difficult (sensitive and light) to take off and land, especially on the troubled seas which were commonly encountered at Yarmouth. There was the danger of smashed airscrews before getting up speed ; the danger of turning turtle on gaining speed and alighting. One was always drenched with spray. They were good machines in the air, but with bombs and other gear it was unwise to load them too much. They had no sights for bombing, but a Lewis machine-gun firing through the airscrew and one also on the top plane. A carrier-pigeon, fresh water and a sea anchor were carried as well.

" The duties of the Schneider Flight (at Yarmouth) were extraordinary in their variety. It was the machine for the lover of solitude and independence and a wandering kind of life. The Schneider was a sort of detective, exposing all mysteries, such as whales mistaken for submarines, streaks of oil, and rescuing colleagues in difficulties. Any wild rumour—out went the Schneider to investigate. They were the police force of the Yarmouth Patrol.

" The question is often asked : How would the Schneider in the hands of a seasoned Schneider pilot have fared in a scrap with a German seaplane ? The Schneider had no sensational accomplishments to its name at Yarmouth, probably because of the amazing way in which it escaped actual contact with the enemy. Perhaps the lonely forager was often seen—unknown to himself— but left alone because of sympathy or fear ! The Schneider patrols usually lasted from one and a half to two hours. The height at which the patrols were made was comparatively low, for experience went to show that small objects, such as periscopes, could not be detected from an 'enclosed' machine like the Schneider from great altitudes, and detection from above of a low-flying Schneider was extremely difficult."

Some figures as to the size and performance of the Sopwith Baby fitted with the 130 h.p. Clergêt are interesting. The span was 25 ft. 8 in., the length 23 ft. and the height 10 ft. The weight of the machine empty was 1,226 lb., loaded it was 1,715 lb., the disposable load being 255 lb. The maximum speed attainable low down was some 98 m.p.h., while the climb to 10,000 feet took 35 minutes.

In Leonard Bridgman's picture the Sopwith Baby which is shown carries an upward-firing gun, and is seen flying over a dazzle-painted patrol gunboat of the " Kil " class—so called because all the eighty-odd ships of this class had names beginning with these three letters.

THE SOPWITH DOLPHIN

View or outlook was the constant preoccupation of British designers during the War. Some believe that excessive emphasis was placed by the air service authorities of that time on view, but at any rate the leading British designers were stimulated to do everything possible to give the pilots of fighting aeroplanes unrestricted outlook. Examples of tractor aeroplanes, in which some major feature of design was determined by the need for unrestricted outlook are the Sopwith Triplane, the D.H.5 and the Sopwith Dolphin, which is the subject of the present commentary.

In general layout the Sopwith Dolphin was extraordinary, but, as can be seen from the illustration, it was not an ugly aeroplane, and it certainly looked like an efficient fighting machine. It will be noticed first of all that the pilot is seated with his head actually in the top centre section, which is in skeleton. The consequence is that the hemisphere above can be completely scanned. Forwards and downwards the outlook is more restricted, but the line from the pilot's eyes downwards over the nose is sloped at a fairly steep angle, and his head comes almost directly over the leading edge of the lower plane.

Consequently, although the Dolphin gave the best possible outlook upwards, it also gave reasonably good outlook forwards and downwards. To the rear and downwards the view was less good, because the lower plane got in the way as well as the fuselage and radiator. The wings had a slight backward stagger, and in this the Dolphin resembled the D.H.5. The gap was large and the fuselage deep. The two Vickers guns were mounted directly in front of the pilot's face and fired forwards in the line of flight through the disc swept by the airscrew. Hydraulic interrupter gear to prevent the bullets hitting the airscrew blades was used. Two Lewis guns were also used in some Dolphins mounted on the steel tube which formed a prolongation of the upper plane main spar. The butts came on either side of the pilot's face. One Dolphin squadron mounted two Lewis guns on the lower wings. They carried one tray of ammunition each, and could not be reloaded in the air ; they were splayed slightly outwards. The Dolphin in this form was a four-gun fighter.

The engine was the geared Hispano-Suiza, and the performance

THE SOPWITH DOLPHIN

of the aeroplane was satisfactory considering how markedly the designers had concentrated upon giving the pilot the best possible outlook. A top speed of about 130 m.p.h. was secured.

One of the earliest Dolphins to reach the Royal Flying Corps was brought to an experimental station where the present writer was serving at the time by Mr. H. T. Tizard (now Sir Henry Tizard) Chairman of the Aeronautical Research Committee, who was a capable pilot. The aeroplane was handed over so that it might be tried in mock combat with a view to estimating its handling qualities and the value of the good outlook. On getting into the cockpit the writer's first remark was, " This would be an unpleasant machine in which to turn over on the ground."

That remark is recorded because it expressed a thought which passed through the heads of almost all the pilots who flew the machine and led to one or two minor modifications. The pilot's head came above the top plane, and he was completely surrounded by longerons, spars, cross-bracing wires and tie rods, and the feeling of being boxed in with the head exposed in a vulnerable position was experienced at once. With the engine in his lap and the petrol tanks in the small of his back, it seemed to the pilot that he had little chance of escaping injury in the event of a bad landing.

Turning over on the ground was not an uncommon form of accident, for a great many aerodromes were in regular use in which the surface was rough. Moreover, the wing loading of the aeroplanes of that time was low so that they were blown over easily on the ground if they were flown as they frequently had to be flown on war service, in high winds. So the anxiety about being boxed in and receiving a crack on the head as the machine turned over on the ground was not entirely without foundation.

As a result some Dolphins were fitted with a " rolling hoop," which went over the pilot's cockpit, and although it slightly impaired his upwards view it gave him an added sense of security, for he felt that the aeroplane could turn over on the ground without his neck getting broken. But that still did not satisfy all pilots, and a subsequent development was a quick release arrangement at the side which theoretically permitted a pilot to open the side of the cockpit and get out if the machine turned over on the ground.

Whether any of these devices were of value or not I do not know. They certainly served their purpose of removing a feeling of anxiety until such time as pilots became familiar with the Dolphin and forgot about its special features and treated it just like any other aeroplane. Those who did not fly in these aeroplanes dreaded having to, but those who got used to them found them warm and comfortable, and were enthusiastic about their good qualities

F

as a fighting machine. Invariably the two Lewis guns which, as has been previously mentioned, were very close to the pilot's face, were mounted elsewhere since they were found difficult to operate in this position and were apt to strike the pilot in the face during intricate manœuvres. Several squadrons received Dolphins, and good work was done with these machines, although they were never used in the quantities of some of the other single-seater fighter types.

Especially valuable, according to Dolphin pilots, was the upward view when engaged in the circular chase type of combat. In this the two machines circle round and round, each trying to get on the other's tail. With the normal biplane with the full centre-section the other aeroplane is frequently out of sight, blocked from view by the pilot's own aeroplane's centre-section and top plane. With the Dolphin the other aeroplane could be watched all the time with a consequent gain in tactical manœuvring.

On the controls the Dolphin, though not showing any great sensitivity, was satisfactory and reasonably well balanced. There were rumours and counter-rumours about it at first, but in fact the machine showed itself to be fairly well balanced on the controls. Sir Henry Tizard, who has been mentioned as flying the first Dolphin to Orfordness, also flew the first one to France. Its silhouette was unfamiliar to the British anti-aircraft gunners who, acting apparently on the rule " if in doubt, shoot," gave Sir Henry a rousing welcome of high explosive and shrapnel.

THE SOPWITH SNIPE

The Sopwith Snipe was the successor to the Sopwith Camel and marked the closing stages of a certain formula in the single-seater fighter design.   It was being issued to fighter squadrons at the end of the war of 1914, and three squadrons were equipped with it ; but its chief claim to attention is as the standard single-seater fighter of the Royal Air Force in the period which immediately followed the war.

Although obviously " Sopwith " in line, the Snipe was a very different aeroplane from the Camel.   It was, if I may so express it, soberer and more dignified.   It was more powerful and it had a better all-round performance, but it had none of the qualities of lightning manœuvre of the Camel.   To turn from a Camel to a Snipe was like turning from an eight horse power sports car to an eight-ton lorry.   The lorry is the more powerful, and it carries more and is bigger ; the eight horse power sports car is lighter and more responsive.

It must not be thought, however, that the Snipe was unpopular. On the contrary it was widely liked by Royal Air Force pilots and, although not suited to aerobatics in the way the Camel was suited to them, it was used for them a great deal, and at many of the Royal Air Force Hendon Pageants (as they were still called at that time) the Snipe was the chief exhibition aeroplane.

Perhaps the difference in the control qualities of these two types may be best expressed by pointing out that the Camel could be flick-rolled at a touch, whereas it was only with a good deal of difficulty and a certain amount of force that the Snipe could be flick-rolled.   Possibly the marked dihedral angle had something to do with it.   And it is instructive to note that the time the Snipe came into use coincided with the time the flick roll went out of use. Gradually it was held to " put a strain on the machine " and then to be " bad flying."   And when aeroplanes were in use which demanded force for flick rolling and only did a flick roll reluctantly, with their pilots whipping them all the way round, there was something to be said for the convention that flick rolling was " bad flying."   But in the days of the super-sensitive type of aeroplane there was nothing " bad " about flick rolling.

A Camel could be flick-rolled all day and every day by a pilot

THE SOPWITH SNIPE

who knew it and knew how to do the manœuvre without the slightest sign of an effect upon the rigging. Actually certain small aeroplanes to-day can be flick-rolled without any excessive strain being put upon them. It is largely a matter of elevator power. With a really powerful elevator and a pilot who knows how to employ it with discretion flick rolling is a legitimate aerobatic. But with an elevator like a ton of bricks flick rolling is to be deprecated.

The illustration shows the two-bay arrangement of the Snipe wings and the generally orthodox formula. The machine shown has the horn ailerons; others had straight ailerons. The centre section was drastically cut away for view. A point of special interest is the rounded fuselage. This is the first note in a standard service type of the fuselage shaping which was later to become general. Plywood fairing was employed and the sides of the fuselage with their fabric-covered stringers were carefully merged into the engine cowling.

The armament consisted of two Vickers guns, interrupted, and firing directly forwards through the field swept by the airscrew. The engine was a B.R.2 of 230 h.p., and the speed at 10,000 ft. was 121 m.p.h. and at 15,000 ft. 113 m.p.h. Ten thousand feet was reached in 9·4 minutes, and 15,000 ft. in 18·8 minutes. The weight loaded was 2,020 lb., and the Snipe carried 38½ gallons of petrol and 7 gallons of oil. As single-seater aeroplanes go to-day the Snipe was not a big machine, but when it appeared it seemed big and, in consequence, it marked an important change in the relationship between the pilot and his aeroplane.

We began to move away from the conception of pilot and aeroplane being one—of rider and horse relationship—and to go towards the captain and ship relationship. It is true to say that the pilot of a modern single-seater fighter directs his machine, whereas the pilots of the early war period—single-seater fighters, or " scouts " as they were called—*handled* their machines. The connection between pilot and machine is becoming less and less direct.

At the time of the early aeroplanes there was a great deal of talk about " hands " and a person with " hands " it was said, made a good pilot, whereas one without this mysterious quality could never fly really well. The Snipe took something away of that direct touch and set the pilot up in a machine which exhibited none of the super-sensitiveness of the Camel ; none of the one-sidedness of the D.H.2 ; none of the elegance and lightness of the Pup ; none of the responsiveness of the Nieuport.

The Snipe gave us the first approach to the flying machine in which the pilot sits up and takes notice, but does not perform a sort of highly skilled balancing act. It paved the way to the elaborate contraptions of to-day in which speed has taken the place of lightning manœuvre and everything is done at second hand through hydraulic and other intermediaries.

Structurally, the Snipe remained true to the original formula, apart from the rounding of the fuselage which has already been mentioned. But the box girder remained the basis of the construction with the biplane form braced with streamline wires. The undercarriage also followed the well-tried formula.

THE NIEUPORT SCOUT

The thing that first catches the eye in this drawing of a Nieuport Scout is the fifth of November effect on the interplane struts. It is the result of the fitting of Le Prieur rockets and before dealing with the Nieuport Scout itself, one of the most interesting types of war machine, I propose to say something of these rockets.

Invented by a French naval officer, Lieutenant Y. P. G. Le Prieur, for shooting down balloons, the rockets were mounted as shown, pointing forward and upward, and they were electrically fired. The idea was that the balloon should be approached to point-blank range and the rockets then released. On the day preceding the Somme offensive of 1916 the Le Prieur rockets were used with success. On the Fourth Army front there were four German observation balloons and it was arranged that they should be subjected to a simultaneous attack at 4 o'clock in the evening.

Almost to the minute three of the balloons were brought down in flames. The attack had been a surprise and had been successful. Afterwards it was decided, for various reasons, that the Le Prieur rocket was less effective for attacking balloons than the ordinary incendiary machine-gun bullet known as the " Buckingham," and, in subsequent attacks, this bullet was used. Le Prieur rockets were not used against Zeppelins in the defence of London.

The Nieuport Scout was a machine of French design which proved one of the most effective fighters of the war and which was used by many of the most successful pilots. The unequal plane arrangement was always popular with the French and was used by them right up to the time when the monoplane began to oust the biplane. They used it not only for their small, but also for their large machines. The Nieuport was among the first to introduce it.

Note the way in which the stagger effect is secured by means of the slope of the V struts which bring the leading edge of the top plane well in advance of the leading edge of the lower plane. The lower plane is of very narrow chord and this aeroplane, like the Sopwith triplane, was credited—whether rightly or wrongly never clearly emerged—with twisting its lower plane round its single spar in a steep dive and becoming as a result uncontrollable.

It is probable that this fault did develop on at least one occasion,

70

THE NIEUPORT SCOUT

but whether as a result of any inherent defect in the design, or for some other reason it is impossible to say. Like other French single-seater fighters the Nieuport Scout was exceedingly pleasant to fly and very handy on the controls. It gave a splendid outlook, especially in a downwards direction.

Fitted with various different engines, the performance of the Nieuport varied with them. It had at first the 110 h.p. Le Rhône and with this the maximum speed was 105 m.p.h. Later the 130 h.p. Clergêt was fitted and, about 1917–18, a Nieuport Scout, built almost to the original formula, was produced with the Hispano-Suiza engine. As will be seen by reference to the commentary on the Sopwith Pup, the Nieuport speed with a 110 h.p. engine was about the same as that achieved by the Pup with an 80 h.p. engine. But it is to be remembered that the Nieuport had qualities which the Pup had not and that the speed went up to over 110 m.p.h. with the bigger engines. The outlook was better and it probably handled more quickly when flying near the ground than the Pup. The Nieuport climbed to 10,000 ft. in $10\frac{1}{2}$ minutes.

The Nieuport's powers of manœuvre near the ground were really remarkable and one of the amusements at an aerodrome on which there were a Sopwith Pup Squadron and a Nieuport Squadron was that of hedge-hopping about the country when there was nothing else to do in the evenings. Pup and Nieuport would compete in a sort of chase over the countryside, all done at a few feet above the grass and the tree-tops, the machines literally jumping over fences and bushes. On these occasions the Nieuport usually proved itself superior.

The armament of the Nieuport Scout went through a series of changes as armament schemes developed. At first, in 1916, during the Le Prieur rocket period and before the introduction of the interrupter gear, a single Lewis gun was mounted above the top wing on brackets to enable it to fire clear of the airscrew. Captain H. A. Cooper and Sergeant Foster of No. 11 Squadron developed the Foster adjustable gun mounting which, later, was used on all kinds of single-seater fighters. With this mounting the gun could be brought down on a curved rail for reloading and upward firing. It could be fired in any position by a Bowden cable.

Albert Ball, perhaps the greatest of all British fighting pilots, achieved his early successes with the Nieuport Scout with the Foster gun mounting. And in fact he adapted his technique for the use of this mounting, attacking enemy machines from below and behind and coming up close to them before opening fire. Ball actually had the second of these mountings to be used in France.

The Nieuport Scout soon gained Ball's confidence. His way of describing it in a letter home was expressive : " It is T.T.," he wrote, " so Huns, *look out*." No. 11 Squadron, which started the Nieuport Scout on its way to fame, was commanded at the time by Major T. O'B. Hubbard, and the only balloon Ball ever brought down was destroyed by him when he was flying a Nieuport. He was certainly fond of his Nieuport, for when they were inferior in performance to both Allied and hostile machines and S.E.5s were issued to his squadron, he appealed to General Trenchard for permission to retain his Nieuport. The outcome of his appeal was that he was given two machines—an S.E.5 for his ordinary work and a Nieuport for his individual enterprises. Of Ball and his Nieuport the Official History of the War in the Air says that they were " the spearhead of the achievement of the Flying Corps over the Somme."

Control of the 110 h.p. Le Rhône was the same in the Nieuport as in other types. It consisted of a " throttle " and a fine adjustment. Some of the fine adjustments were of the screw type and others of the lever type and in later models a device was used which enabled the engine to be controlled to a large extent by one lever. But mainly it was necessary to use both the fine adjustment and the throttle to set the engine revolutions. When approaching prior to landing the thumb switch on the stick or on the dash had also to be used.

Inexperienced pilots had a good deal of trouble with this form of control, for the 110 h.p. Le Rhône choked easily if the fine adjustment were not correctly used. The system was for the engine to be run up and the fine adjustment to be closed gradually until the revolutions dropped and perhaps an occasional misfire set in. This indicated that the mixture had been weakened beyond the even-firing limit and the fine adjustment was then opened slightly to let the engine pick up to full revolutions again.

The pilot now noted the position of the fine adjustment screw and closed it down a good deal while he used the switch and " blipped " the engine while taxi-ing out for the take-off. If he did not close the fine adjustment down while taxi-ing, the engine would collect a too rich mixture and there would be a risk of it choking when he opened up to take off. Still more unsatisfactory would be the circumstances if the pilot did not note the correct full throttle position for the fine adjustment and, when taking off, turned it too far open. In that case the engine might run all right at first and then cut out, choked, as the machine got off the ground.

For " dog fighting " of the most intensive kind, when aeroplanes whirled about within inches of each other, it is doubtful if there was ever a better machine than the Nieuport Scout. It not only had the quickness of control, but it also had the good outlook given by the narrow lower plane, a feature copied by the Germans in the later Albatross and Pfaltz Scouts. Possibly its range of aerobatics was more limited than that of the Camel ; but the Camel's wider lower plane reduced its outlook. One gained where the other lost.

THE MARTINSYDE ELEPHANT

Exactly why the Martinsyde scout was called an elephant is difficult to discover. At any rate, although the aeroplane did have an appearance of great solidity and strength, it had little else to connect it with an elephant. As a single-seater scout the original Martinsyde started life in 1915 fitted with a 120 h.p. Beardmore engine and formed the original active service equipment of No. 27 Squadron of the Royal Flying Corps. The armament was two Lewis guns, one on top of the centre section, firing over the airscrew disc, and the other on a mounting on the starboard side of the fuselage in line with the rear edge of the cockpit. The second gun was for firing backwards.

Later, in 1916, the Martinsyde scout was fitted with the 160 h.p. Beardmore engine and it seems that it was about this time that it got its name as the Elephant. It also underwent a conversion from a pure single-seater fighter, to a fighter-bomber. Leonard Bridgman's picture shows the Martinsyde Elephant in this form, with its single 112 lb. bomb slung in the rack under the fuselage and just aft of the undercarriage.

A top speed of between 90 and 95 m.p.h. was obtained with the Martinsyde Elephant and the aeroplane had a wing span of 33 ft. 8 in. and a length of 25 ft. 4 in. It was a production of the famous pioneer firm of Martin and Handasyde and was the fore-runner of the Martinsyde F4 which acquired a big reputation for speed. Mr. Handasyde started designing aeroplanes in 1908.

As a flying machine the Martinsyde Elephant had many pleasing qualities. It ambled through the air with a rather gentle burbling sound and seemed to get about the country fairly quickly. The outlook from the pilot's cockpit was somewhat restricted and the present writer, when he once got lost in one of these aeroplanes on a day when rain was falling and visibility was bad, found the restricted forward outlook made it difficult to recognize landmarks. But the flying quality which was chiefly attributed to this machine by the pilots of the period was that of " floating " when landing.

Actually floating must be regarded as the responsibility partly of the pilot and partly of the aeroplane. In so far as the aeroplane is responsible, it is a testimony to sound design ; for the cleaner the design, the greater the float after the approach at a given speed.

74

THE MARTINSYDE ELEPHANT

The war-time machines were mostly far from clean. The biplane does not lend itself to really clean design and there were the struts and bracing wires all contributing to the drag. Pusher aeroplanes, especially, had almost no float because directly power was cut off and the aeroplane tilted for the touch down, the drag pulled it up like a powerful air brake.

When a relatively clean design like the Martinsyde Elephant came out, pilots used to things that stood still and dropped the moment the stick was brought back, were a little puzzled by it. If they approached in their habitual manner, with a big margin of speed over stalling speed, they found the machine shooting across the aerodrome towards the opposite hedge at the moment when they expected it to be sitting down on the grass.

It was, as I say, an excellent quality in the aeroplane because it demonstrated low drag. But at that time—and even on occasions to-day—pilots talk about it as if it were a fault. So the word went round that the Martinsyde Elephant " floated badly." I suppose the reputation of the machine was slightly damaged by this story. But in fact, directly one became familiar with the Martinsyde, or indeed with any other aeroplane with the reputation for floating, one found that the float could be prevented and the landing made in a short space provided only that the approach was adjusted so that only a small margin of speed over the landing speed was maintained.

In the modern aeroplane, floating would indeed be a fault if there were no provision for checking it. The cleaning up has been carried so far that the margin between approach speed and landing speed would have to be reduced below the practicable limit in order to prevent float if there were no such things as air brakes. But in fact the retractable undercarriage and wing flap act as air brakes and turn a clean, low drag machine into a less clean, higher-drag machine which can be brought down in the orthodox manner, with a fairly big margin of speed over the stalling speed, in the approach, but which will touch down soon enough after the flattening-out process has begun.

So when we remember that the Martinsyde Elephant had this reputation for floating we remember a strong testimony in favour of the excellence of the design. As for the controls of the Martinsyde Elephant, they were reasonably good although the ailerons failed to produce as quick or as big a response as many pilots would have liked and the elevator had none of the sensitivity of the elevator, for instance, of a Camel.

The only serious fault was the poor outlook. The pilot sat just behind the trailing edge of the top plane with the trailing edge of the lower plane almost immediately below him. Forwards and upwards a big arc of view was blanked out by the top plane and downwards and forwards there was another big arc of view blanked out. The big chord of the wings added to the blanking effect. In addition, the forward part of the fuselage, and the cowling of the Beardmore engine, came rather high and still further restricted the forward outlook.

The Martinsyde was used not only in France, but also in Mesopotamia, Palestine and Macedonia. It is of interest to note that No. 27 Squadron of the Royal Air Force bears on its crest even to-day an elephant which recalls to those who are familiar with the squadron's history the start of its career in the Royal Flying Corps and the first aeroplanes with which it was equipped for active service.

THE MARTINSYDE F.4

Showing clearly its descent from the Martinsyde Elephant, the Martinsyde F.4 marked an important step towards the bigger, higher-powered, high speed aeroplane for single-seater fighter purposes. It came just before there was a determined effort to reduce the size and power of single-seaters and to introduce the very small, highly manœuvrable machine in place of the bigger, faster but usually less manœuvrable type.

The Martinsyde bore the same sort of relationship to things like the B.A.T. Bantam that the train bears to the motor-car. It could get going at an extremely high speed, but it had to move straight, or in curves of big radius. There was none of the jumpy quickness of the Bantam about it. It was in almost every respect like an express train. It went tearing along at high speed with the pilot sitting in a comfortable cockpit which enclosed him enough to keep the draughts away. There was a faint rumbling in front from the Hispano-Suiza engine or, in the earlier type, the Rolls-Royce engine.

A fine machine in which to do long cross-country flights ; with Pullman car effects the Martinsyde achieved a high reputation. Its top speed was rather over 145 m.p.h. It was also respected for competence—though not exactly for quickness—on the controls. It could be made to do the usual range of aerobatics, and its loops were impressively train-like ; it went roaring up the incline leaving behind it the appropriate trail of smoke, and came coasting down again on the other side as if it were running into a station.

Once it actually did run into a station when it was being looped very low during a display of aerobatics by a distinguished and highly skilled officer of the Royal Air Force. He came rushing down the incline in readiness for his loop and determined to get as near the ground as possible before starting it. The speed rose to a very high figure, but the machine itself went a fraction too low. The undercarriage caught the ground and melted away to a sound like a French express train going through a tunnel. The Martinsyde slid along on its belly and came to rest. The pilot got out and went and had tea. The only remarks he was ever heard to make about the incident are not suitable for reproduction.

THE MARTINSYDE F.4

The wing span of the Martinsyde F.4 was 32 ft. 9 in., the length 25 ft. 9 in. and the height 9 ft. When fully loaded it weighed 2,550 lb., and at 10,000 ft. the speed was 142·5 m.p.h. The climb to 10,000 ft. took 8 minutes, and to 20,000 ft., where this aeroplane was quite happy, 28 minutes. The ceiling was 22,000 ft. and the range 2½ hours.

The Martinsyde F.4 foreshadowed the single-seater aeroplane of to-day, which is somewhat train-like in that it possesses an enormously high top speed, and is extremely clean, so that its momentum has the sort of effect it has on a train. Once get the machine moving and it takes a lot to stop it. Its movement is essentially train-like, and although the controls are extremely effective, the cleanness and the high top speed itself must be paid for by a diminution in the suddenness with which manœuvres can be done and in the quickness with which the machine may be deflected from its course.

Constructionally the Martinsyde kept to the tradition set up by the B.Es. It was of wood, wire and fabric. The outlook from the pilot's seat was not particularly good, but it was probably better than from the pilot's cockpit of the old Martinsyde Elephant. Two guns firing forward in the line of flight were to have been its armament.

THE BRISTOL D SCOUT

The Bristol Scout or Bullet was another of those fine flying machines which were never able to exert their full military significance because of unsuitable armament. It was built in 1914, and two machines of this type went to France in September, 1914, so that it may be grouped among the earliest scouts in use in the flying service. But it did not even have a Lewis gun on a Foster mounting and it certainly had no Vickers gun.

In fact the armament of a great many of the Bristol Scouts used in the early stages of the War consisted of the revolver of the pilot. Later on a machine gun was sometimes rigged up beside the fuselage at such an angle that the bullets went clear of the disc swept by the airscrew. Every squadron, in those early days, was supposed to incorporate its own arrangements for defence, and consequently the Bristol Scouts were scattered about the squadrons, each squadron having one or two of them.

A delightful aeroplane to fly, the Bristol Scout's most noticeable feature was its square-shaped rudder. This was balanced, and was powerful without being unduly sensitive. The fuselage was rather low and narrow, so that the pilot felt as if he were sitting mainly outside the machine, and this gave him the impression of having an exceptionally good outlook. Another good thing about the Bristol Scout, from the pilot's point of view, was the seeming stiffness of the wing cells and structure in general.

There was never the slightest suggestion of " flap " or give during the most vigorously executed manœuvres such as engine-on flick rolls. The small span wings with their steep-angled flying wires and landing wires seemed very rigid. On landing the effect of the behaviour of the machine was to suggest a rather unusually far-back centre of gravity relative to the points of contact of the wheels. And this again made for confidence when landing.

It is true that if the centre of gravity is brought far enough back there may be a tendency for an aeroplane to buck if the tail-skid touches before the wheels, but even this tendency was preferred by most pilots to nose-heaviness on the ground. Moreover, with correct procedure the aeroplane with the far-back centre of gravity can be kept from bucking and landed in an orthodox manner.

Things to notice about the Bristol Scout are the classic simplicity

THE BRISTOL D SCOUT

of the line ; the neat engine cowling, the short stiff wing-bays and the wing-tip skids. The undercarriage track is fairly narrow so that the wing-tip skids were needed to prevent damage when the machine was being landed in a high wind.

Various engines were fitted to the Bristol Scout. The first was the 80 h.p. Gnôme, and after that the 80 h.p. Le Rhône was fitted. Perhaps the machine was at its best as a flying machine with this delightful little engine. But it had other higher-powered engines also fitted, among them the 100 h.p. Monosoupape, the 110 h.p. Le Rhône and the 130 h.p. Clergêt. With the 80 h.p. Gnôme the top speed was 86 m.p.h. ; with the 80 h.p. Le Rhône it was 94 m.p.h., and with the Monosoupape 104 m.p.h. At first it had no gun, but later a gun was fitted firing through the field swept by the airscrew and mounted on top of the fuselage just inside the port centre section struts. After it had been superseded as a war machine, the Bristol Scout was extensively used by the Royal Naval Air Service for training.

Incidentally, the energy with which officers of high enough rank pursued Bristol Scouts after their period of war-usefulness was over, in order to husband them to their squadrons as " training " machines, was in itself high testimony to the popularity among pilots of this little aeroplane. A pilot who was able to secure one of these aeroplanes was looked upon with envy by all other pilots, and he would take very good care that his " training " machine was never used for training and that no pilot but himself ever went near it.

I have often wondered how a modern flying club would appreciate a Bristol Scout with 80 h.p. Le Rhône or a Sopwith Pup with 80 h.p. Le Rhône. I believe that these machines would exercise to-day over the members of a flying club just as strong a fascination as they exercised over the Royal Flying Corps and Royal Naval Air Service pilots during the War. They were both great flying machines, and although of the two the Sopwith Pup was probably superior, they both gave their pilots the authentic sensations of man-controlled flight in a way that few, if any, other machines have ever done.

THE BRISTOL MONOPLANE

" Bristol Monoplane." These were the words that brought hope and encouragement to many a war pilot. They suggested a fighting machine so far superior to anything possessed by the enemy that they would be able to achieve dominance without great risk. Rumours flew about this machine in rather the way they did with the D.H.4 and the Martinsyde Scout before they came into service. And as the rumours flew, so they grew. The little Bristol Monoplane, admittedly a brilliant piece of design and far in advance of its period in many respects, was endowed with Spitfire qualities. Prodigious speeds were quoted as being within its reach, and prodigious powers of manœuvre. It was eagerly awaited. The prospect of getting it and using it over the lines buoyed up the fighting pilots, and especially those who were under the disadvantage of working with inferior quality machines.

There was something almost tragic in the way the pilots waited and the way the rumours grew to a maximum and then began to fade. I am not going to judge those whose duty it was to select and order aeroplanes for the flying services, but I am going to give the impression which obtained in countless Royal Flying Corps messes in France about the Bristol Monoplane. It was believed that this aeroplane would have conferred upon British pilots a tactical superiority through the medium of a considerable excess of speed and climb over the aeroplanes of the enemy, and there seems little doubt that the Bristol Monoplane, although it came out much earlier than the S.E. or the Snipe, was actually superior to both of them in all-round performance and powers of manœuvre. With the 110 Le Rhône engine its top speed was 130 to 135 m.p.h., slightly below that of the higher-powered S.Es. but above that of the Snipe, and it climbed to 10,000 ft. in nine minutes which was again better than the Snipe aeroplane, with which the flying service was equipped after the War, could do.

Here, then, was an aeroplane with a fixed Vickers gun firing forwards through the field swept by the airscrew, with a performance so far superior to that of any of its contemporaries that it would have given our pilots psychological and physical ascendancy of the most convincing kind. Why was it never adopted for the Royal Flying Corps in France ? Why was such an outstanding

G

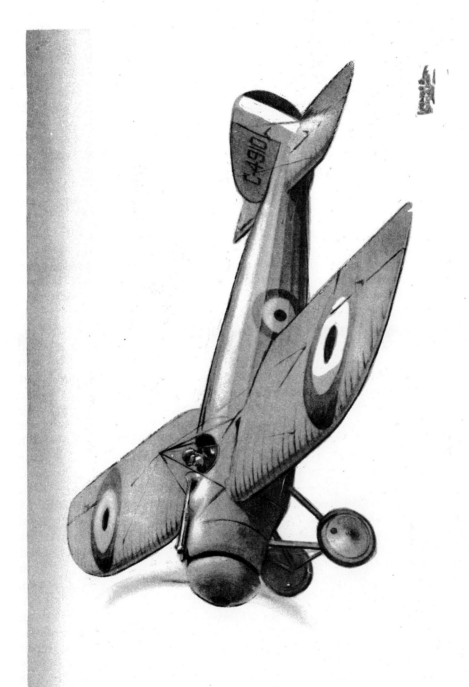

THE BRISTOL MONOPLANE

type, without vices so far as the present writer could ascertain, and with every desirable quality, only ordered to an insignificant extent and then sent to serve in Palestine, Mesopotamia and Macedonia ?

I do not know the official answers to these questions. The answers which were given in the Royal Flying Corps messes were not flattering to the authorities. It was first said that the aeroplane was condemned as a big production machine for France because the outlook down and forward was too much restricted by the monoplane wings. This was an argument whose futility could only be fully appreciated by pilots who had seen the staff striving for a long time so to modify and hack about every service aeroplane as to give unrestricted upwards and forwards view. The D.H.5 and the way in which Camel centre-sections were slashed about, the Sopwith Dolphin and even the S.E.5 arrangement, were all aimed at giving good upward and forward outlook. Yet the Bristol Monoplane, which gave better upward and forward view than any of them, was said to have been condemned because it did not give downward and forward view.

It is true that the downward and forward view was slightly restricted, but there was not a fighting pilot of experience who would not have exchanged that view for the speed and climb of the Bristol Monoplane with alacrity and enthusiasm. There was reason to suppose that the authorities were placing an altogether unjustifiable amount of importance upon view in certain directions and were neglecting more truly important qualities. One other reason which the authorities were supposed to have adduced for not putting the Bristol Monoplane into service in France, was that it was " difficult to fly." This view had no foundation in fact. The Bristol Monoplane was as easy to fly as any comparable type, and had no vices.

If the picture of this aeroplane is examined it will be seen that a great many things which are now regarded as essential to the up-to-date aeroplane were included in the Bristol Monoplane. The low-drag cowling, for instance, bears a close likeness to the modern low-drag cowlings, and the wing shape, with the considerable taper, resembles modern wing shapes. In fact the Bristol Monoplane is one of those machines which contribute the evidence for the outstanding conclusion to which anyone who studies the types which are dealt with in this book must come—that almost everything in the way of design and constructional technique was tried between the day when the first flight was made and the day when the war ended. The thoughts of designers and pilots preceded the achievements. Captain Barnwell, when he planned the Bristol Monoplane of the war period, looked ahead as clearly as Pégoud looked ahead—he in designing, the other in piloting.

That is why the Bristol Monoplane holds a place in aeronautical history of much greater eminence than would be supposed from the number built and the amount they were used. It is a machine which showed the trend of advanced design thought. Had it been adopted for large-scale series production for use on the Western Front there is little doubt that it would have achieved a fighting reputation as good as its design reputation. But like many advanced types, those in authority regarded it with suspicion and would not give it their unqualified approval. Subsequent critics have spent a lot of time righting that wrong and giving the Bristol Monoplane the praise it so richly merited.

THE BRISTOL FIGHTER

Strictly speaking, the Bristol Fighter should be spoken of in terms of the heroes of classical mythology. It was, in the fullest sense, a hero after their pattern—a fighter by name, inclination and aptitude. Look at this picture of the Bristol Fighter. Two men are tied together, back to back, in the narrow cockpits. Each is furnished with a gun which he can wield in front of him. For the rest the aeroplane has the smallest possible quantity of wings, wires and wood and is so disposed about the men that it interferes as little as possible with their outlook and their gunnery. Add also the fullest powers of manœuvre and enormous strength. This was the aeroplane which Captain Barnwell produced and which, in March, 1917, went to the rescue of the hard-pressed squadrons of the Royal Flying Corps in France.

Furnished with the Rolls-Royce Falcon III engine of 250 h.p., the Bristol Fighter had a total all-up weight of 2,800 lb. and was loaded at 6·92 lb. per square foot of wing area. At 10,000 ft. it did 102 m.p.h. and at 15,000 ft. 88 m.p.h. It could climb to 10,000 ft. with full military load in 17·5 minutes and to 15,000 ft. in 42 minutes. Apart from fuel the disposable load was 630 lb. These figures however, were by no means final and in slightly modified form, but still with Rolls-Royce engine, the speed at 10,000 ft. went up to 113 m.p.h. and at sea level it was about 125 m.p.h., while the climb to 10,000 ft. could be completed in 11 minutes. With a 300 h.p. B.H.P. engine the Bristol Fighter did 20,000 ft. in 20 minutes, but in this form it never saw service. The wing span was 39 ft. 3 in., the length 25 ft. 9 in. and the height 10 ft. 1 in. The wing chord was 5 ft. 6 in.

In this relatively small aeroplane, with pilot and observer crammed close together in the fabric-covered distinctively rectangular fuselage, some of the greatest combats of the War were fought. There were no odds which the Bristol Fighters refused to tackle. The pilot, sitting behind the trailing-edge of the top plane, with his observer in close touch with him and protecting his back, felt that he could see and manœuvre. The machine seemed to be stripped for action, carrying nothing in the way of useless equipment. The way in which the fuselage was slung, half-way between the upper and lower planes, accentuated the stripped-for-action

THE BRISTOL FIGHTER

effect and set out the crew on a sort of all-way observation tower. A pilot so placed could go into action with confidence. His back was protected and he could concentrate upon bringing his front fixed Vickers gun into action. This fired through the field swept by the airscrew and was worked by the Constantinesco hydraulic interrupter gear. The observer had a pair of Lewis guns on a Scarff mounting.

The method of fighting a Fighter was the subject of a good deal of discussion when it first appeared. The chief question at issue was whether the pilot should seek to place his aeroplane so as to give his observer an opportunity for shooting and reserve the front gun for emergency purposes ; or whether he should fight the machine as a single-seater, seeking always to attack with his front gun and leave the observer the task of beating off any machines that might attack from the rear with gun fire. The problem was wrapped up with the comparative performance of the Bristol Fighter and the enemy aeroplanes with which it came in contact. Had the performance been less good, the observer's guns might have been used for the attack ; but as it was the method generally adopted was that of using the front gun, fighting the machine always as a single-seater, and regarding the observer as a sort of armour against attack from the rear. The high speed—for the time—the powers of manœuvre and the immense strength of the Bristol Fighter, ministered to this form of tactics.

The pilot could enter a dog-fight and turn almost as quickly and on almost as small a radius as the best single-seater. He could fling his machine about, go into vertical dives, pull it out quickly, turn it on its back, spin it, roll it and generally do every sort of manœuvre if the need arose. And all the time there was the comfortable feeling that the observer was there with his pair of Lewis guns, watching and protecting. It is not to be wondered at, when one knows this aeroplane and when one has obtained experience of its flying qualities, that the pilots who used the Bristol Fighter were ready to tackle tremendous odds. It is not to be wondered at that the machine came to be dreaded by enemy pilots.

Seventeen squadrons were equipped with Bristol Fighters during the War, and afterwards the aeroplane showed astonishing tenacity of life, for it kept in the Royal Air Force for many years and was one of the last War types to be superseded. It was used for every conceivable duty, for all sorts of experiments, for every flight where good handling qualities were needed. It contributed to the spinning research with full-scale work ; it was used for testing new gun-mountings and gun-sights. It was used for aerobatics by many pilots, who contrived to do in it everything that the single-seater fighters could do. It was used with various engines, including the Hispano-Suiza and the Sunbeam Arab. Structurally there was nothing very unusual about the Bristol Fighter except the way in which the top and bottom of the fuselage were made to come together at the tail with only slight narrowing of the width. There was, in consequence, a horizontal edge to the end of the fuselage. The Fighter had an adjustable tail-plane, and it could be flown with either an observer or ballast in the rear seat.

A large part of the success of the Bristol Fighter must be attributed to the Rolls-Royce Falcon engine, which was one of the pleasantest engines to sit behind ever produced. In the Bristol Fighter it was started with a hand primer and with the aid of a hand magneto. The airscrew had to be swung before the Hucks starter came into general use, and the method was to have two or three men to do the swinging. They linked hands, and the one nearest the airscrew put one hand on the lower blade. The usual orders, " Contact," were exchanged and then the men pulled all together on the airscrew while someone wound the starting magneto.

Many stories are told round the Bristol Fighter, but the thing which ought to be remembered about them above all else was the heroism of the observers. Machines came back from patrol again and again with their observers dead in the rear cockpit, and the casualties among observers were exceptionally high. The reason is to be found in the tactics used. As has been explained, the pilots fought their machines as single-seaters and left the rear defence to the observer. Acts of prodigious courage were entailed in this defence work, for the observer, with no engine to protect him, had often to stand up in his narrow cockpit and face the fire of diving fighters and, at the same time, to attempt to bring effective fire to bear upon them. At such moments the observer's twin Lewis guns must have seemed a poor counter to the fixed guns of the German machines. Yet, in spite of the difficulties and dangers of the observer's task, in spite of the heavy casualties, there was never a lack of volunteers for work with the Bristol Fighters.

It happened, too, on more than one occasion, that the observer found himself in an aeroplane whose pilot had been killed or disabled by enemy fire. He had then to strive to regain control by whatever means he could and to bring the machine safely to the ground. After the War the Bristol Fighter was found to be a delightful aeroplane for cross-country flying, and the present writer used it frequently for travelling down from his station to London to visit motor-car races at Brooklands and occasionally to visit the Country Club which had at that time been established at Hendon.

A big part was played by the Bristol Fighter in influencing tactical development. It was the first two-seater fighter, and it therefore introduced the conception of the fighting aeroplane as a platform for gun positions as opposed to the conception of the aeroplane as a gun with wings. Since the War the Royal Air Force has maintained its interest in two-seater fighters and has usually kept at least one squadron equipped with this type of aeroplane. Foreign countries, notably France, have extended the idea to include twin-engined machines carrying several gun positions. These further developments, however, have not yet been tested on active service, and they depart considerably from the Bristol Fighter conception. In this the aeroplane is looked upon first and last as a single-seater. It is given high performance and high powers of manœuvre, and the rear gunner is added as a protection which should enable that performance and manœuvre to be employed to the best advantage.

It may be asked how it is that, with the historic and successful example of the Bristol Fighter before them, the Royal Air Force authorities have invariably selected the single-seater as the chief fighting type and have never had more than a few two-seater fighters. The answer is to be found in two different parts—the first having to do with supply of equipment and personnel and the second having to do with performance. The two-seater fighter is more expensive than the comparable single-seater fighter not only in money but in the currency which has paramount importance in war time—man-hours. It is also more expensive in personnel, for it calls for two men in place of one and both of these men must be highly skilled in their various tasks.

If the two-seater fighter showed a very marked superiority over the single-seater it is likely that the additional expense of making and manning them would have been accepted. But it is axiomatic that the single-seater fighter has a better performance in speed and climb, and must always and inevitably have a better performance than the two-seater. The proof is that any two-seater fighter can be given a slightly higher top speed and rate of climb merely by taking the observer and his guns out and filling in the cockpit aperture. Consequently the single-seater will always be the better performer and the greater the margin of performance over the two-seater the less the advantage given by the extra man with his pair of guns. These are the reasons why the single-seater is preferred as a practical military machine in spite of the wonderful record of the Bristol Fighter.

THE BRISTOL F

The Bristol F (Sunbeam) looked good. Pilots who saw it liked it ; and the present writer, who not only saw it but who did a good many hours' flying in it, regarded it as an excellent single-seater machine. The only trouble was that the engine was not fully developed in time for the airframe, and the consequence was that engine troubles, frequently concerned with vibration and failure of the bearers, held the aeroplane back from obtaining its full share of credit.

But it was an excellent aeroplane to handle, capable of all the range of aerobatics and able to do them fairly quickly. Probably the thing that strikes the observer of Leonard Bridgman's drawing of the Bristol F with Sunbeam Arab engine to-day, is the resemblance between the line of the front part and that of the Hawker Fury fighters which, in comparatively recent times, had such a long and successful period of service in the Royal Air Force. This streamlined nose at the time of the Bristol F was an innovation. So was the radiator position underneath the engine.

The Spad and the S.E.5, both of them single-seater scouts with stationary, liquid-cooled engines, retained the car convention and stuck their radiators flat in front of the machine, making a blunt entry and a fuselage line which tapered from that blunt entry to the tail. But the Bristol F—and no doubt this was one of the reasons it appealed so strongly to the eye—had the pointed entry and the fuselage line which swelled out towards the pilot's cockpit and then dwindled again towards the tail.

An additional finish was given to this line by the airscrew spinner which completed it and provided the pointed or nearly pointed nose to the whole machine. Other features were the interplane struts, the rather wide gap and the big difference in chord between upper and lower planes. The gap, together with the pointed nose, gave the pilot an excellent outlook. When landing the lower plane came near the ground, and the whole machine stood low when on the ground.

The 200 h.p. Sunbeam Arab was, for its day, a high revving engine, and when it was running well it was a pleasant engine. It was also compact, and it lent itself to mounting in small single-seater machines without spoiling their exterior form. But it is

THE BRISTOL F SCOUT (ARAB)

probably just to say that it was the cause of the Bristol F being one of those types of aeroplane, excellent in themselves, which never went into series production.

For its day the Bristol F scout with Sunbeam Arab was a good performer, for the Martlesham figures credited it with a speed of 128 m.p.h. at 10,000 ft., and it was able to do about 145 m.p.h. when near the ground. The Bristol scout F.1 was a development of the Arab-engined machine, but it was powered with a Cosmos radial air-cooled engine, and this completely altered the external shape and changed the pointed, good-looking entry to a relatively blunt entry. It had a similar plane arrangement with " N " struts and a span of 29 ft. 6 in., and a length of 20 ft. 10 in.

As for the control qualities of the machine, they are best described by saying that they were mid-way between those of the Camel and those of the S.E.5. The elevator was not so sensitive as that of the Camel, but it was probably more powerful than that of the S.E.5. And in general the aeroplane felt handier than the S.E.5, but less handy than the Camel.

The Bristol F was a machine of quality, and although it never came into general use in the Royal Flying Corps or the Royal Naval Air Service, those who flew it will remember it with interest and with a certain amount of admiration. It was not a prodigy, but it was a pleasant aeroplane with many good qualities.

THE S.E.5

If it were possible to estimate the amount of aerial fighting done since the beginning of aviation, it would probably be found that the S.E.5 would come out at the top of the list. This was the single-seater which was in use during the most intensive period of air warfare, in the last eighteen months, when battles between large formations were common and when the fullest use was being made of the air arm not only for bombing, reconnaissance, photography, Army co-operation and fighting, but also for special work such as low-flying attacks on ground troops. The S.E.5 may be regarded as the most successful product of the Royal Aircraft Factory.

A development rather than a design, the S.E. went through various stages of modification and change and was fitted with several different engines ; but its primary characteristic, when it finally came into extensive use, was its high degree—for a single-seater—of automatic stability. It came as near to " flying itself " as could be expected from a small machine with reasonably good control. Inevitably its stability diminished its controllability, and it was much less quick than a Camel or, to take a more truly comparable type, a Spad. But its top speed was higher than that of the Camel, and those who liked it made great play with the theory that it provided a steady gun platform and that, in consequence, enemy aeroplanes could be engaged at greater ranges than they could from less stable but more sensitive machines.

The S.E.5 also earned a reputation for strength, and pilots were ready to dive it steeply and to pull it out of the dive on fairly small radius curves without wondering if the wings would fall off. In the air it had no vices, but at one time there was an epidemic of tippings up on the ground owing to the relationship of the undercarriage wheels and the centre of gravity. The machine tended to be nose-heavy on the ground. There was also the tendency to " swing " when taking off which the S.E.5s with geared Hispano-Suiza engine and four-bladed airscrew exhibited when they were being handled by pilots who were unfamiliar with them. But neither of these faults, if they can be considered as faults, bothered those who got to know the S.E.

The S.E. series began long before the appearance of the S.E.5.

THE S.E.5

The S.E.2, which was the second machine to be designed and built at the Royal Aircraft Factory and the only machine of its type, joined No. 5 Squadron in January, 1914, and was flown by Major Higgins over to France to join No. 3 Squadron in October of that year.   It remained in France until the spring of 1915, and an early staff officer writes : " Its speed enabled it to circle round the enemy's machines and gave it a decided ascendancy."

Fitted with the 80 h.p. Gnôme engine, the S.E.2 was rather similar to the S.E.4, which may be regarded as the direct parent of the S.E.5, except that it had staggered angle bay wings with parallel interplane struts and the B.E. type skid undercarriage. It was in 1914 that the S.E.4 came on the scene, and it was flown by Mr. N. C. Spratt and Sir John Salmond.   It was rather an advanced design and is worth a brief note.   It was a biplane with very little stagger and a rather big gap.   Single interplane struts were used.   The fuselage was of rounded section with a fairing behind the pilot's head and the fin, as in the later machines, was both above and below the fuselage.   But this was before the high aspect ratio controls had become so popular and consequently the rudder was much squarer in shape and had none of the characteristic high, narrow silhouette of the later machine.

The top plane was cut away at the centre section in front and above the pilot.   The undercarriage was a simple V-strut one, cross-braced, with a faired axle and faired strut joints.   The airscrew was furnished with a spinner and was of the four-bladed type. One of the later modifications of the machine gave the pilot a closed cockpit, so that the S.E.4 may be said to have forecast with some degree of accuracy later types of machine.   In addition, it was camouflaged in a pattern vaguely resembling the camouflage now used by the Royal Air Force for its bombing aeroplanes.

Bridgman shows in the main picture the S.E.5 fitted with the 180 h.p. Wolseley Viper engine, which was the third of different types of engine to be standardized.   The first was the 150 h.p. Hispano-Suiza and the second the 200 h.p. Hispano-Suiza, when the aeroplane was known as the S.E.5a.   In this form it had a maximum speed of 132 m.p.h. at 6,500 ft. and could climb to 15,000 ft. in under 23 minutes.   A single Vickers gun was mounted, firing through the field swept by the airscrew, and there was a Lewis gun on the centre section.   Ring sights and an Aldis tube were mounted forward on the windscreen.

The smaller sketch to the right shows the detail of the Foster–Lewis gun-mounting, and in it the fitting of the Aldis tube sight can also be studied.   Another point to be noted in this sketch is the end of one of the twin exhaust pipes.   The S.E.5 was at the time one of the quietest aeroplanes, and the reason lay partly in the use of twin, long exhaust pipes—one on either side of the fuselage, with slit or perforated ends. The upper sketch shows the silhouette which became so well known to large numbers of war pilots. The aeroplane is the S.E.5a with the 200 h.p. Hispano-Suiza engine.

The high aspect ratio rudder will be noticed and the characteristic tail-fin arrangement, above and below the fuselage, a legacy of the early machine which has already been described. The under-carriage is the neat steel strut one. From this sketch, too, an idea can be gained of the outlook. The pilot's eyes are well below the level of the top plane, but the centre section is slightly cut away and the lower plane is well in front of him and at such an angle that it obscures only a relatively small arc. The fuselage was narrow so that view downwards was excellent.

Squadron markings used on the S.E.5s were distinctive. No. 24 Squadron, for instance, had a single white vertical bar on the sides of the fuselage just in front of the cockades. No. 40 had three vertical bars, one on each side of the cockade, and one just forward of the leading edge of the tail plane. No. 41 had two bars, one on each side of the cockade ; No. 84 had a white horizontal bar between cockade and tail plane ; No. 60 had a white disc behind the cockade ; No. 94 had three white vertical bars behind the cockade ; No. 56 had an 18-inch white band round the fuselage just forward of the tail plane ; and No. 1 had a white ring behind the cockade.

The S.E.5 had a span of 26 ft. 8 in., a length of 21 ft. and a height of 9 ft. 6 in. The chord was 5 ft. The weight, empty, was 1,531 lb. and loaded 2,048 lb. A ceiling of 20,000 ft. was obtained. Some twenty squadrons were equipped with S.E.5 machines which went into production in 1917, and some of the best British fighting pilots used them, including McCudden and Mannock. In consequence no aeroplane carries with it a more pronouncedly war-time flavour. Even to-day there are thousands of people to whom the passage of an S.E.5 across the sky and a glimpse of the characteristic fin and rudder and the pronounced wing dihedral would bring many memories. It is of all aeroplanes the richest in the associations of aerial fighting, of hard-contested and long-drawn-out " dog fights," of battles against heavy odds, of extra-ordinary escapes.

Perhaps there is a touch of irony in the task to which the S.E.5 turned, when it was demobilized, at the conclusion of the War. It switched from battle to advertisement, from fighting to writing. It was employed for sky-writing with smoke and it pioneered sky-writing methods. Almost the entire fleet of sky-writing machines

S.E.2

S.E.4

828

THE S.E.2 AND S.E.4

was formed of S.E.5 aeroplanes fitted with the special smoke equipment. They were sufficiently fast, sufficiently easy to fly, and they had a sufficiently high ceiling to fulfil all the needs.

Occasionally an S.E. would appear at race meetings after the War, and then it would still demonstrate a turn of speed and good powers of manœuvre on the turns. One, at least, was privately owned and used for touring. The owner was a doctor living in Canterbury, and his S.E. was looked after by his chauffeur, and he used it extensively for travelling about the country. It appeared, too, in some films which were intended to depict war-time flying. But gradually it faded from the scene, and to-day it is becoming a rarity. For many people the clearest memory of the days of its decline will be the occasion at one of the early Royal Air Force Pageants (as they were then called) at Hendon, when a formation of five S.E.5s under Squadron Leader Noakes gave one of the most spectacular performances of formation aerobatics that has been seen.

THE SPAD

To the French flying service the Spad stood in the same sort of relationship as the S.E.5 to the Royal Flying Corps. And its flying qualities differed as markedly as did the pilots of the R.F.C. from those of the French service. It was an eminently French machine—sensitive, neat, elegant to look at, demanding skill from its pilots and amply repaying the exercise of skill.

I suppose the thing in which the Spad showed most clearly its French origin was in the absence of dihedral. English pilots were taught—erroneously—that a dihedral angle in the wings was essential for stability, and that an aeroplane without a dihedral angle was bound to be vicious and inclined to turn over on its back if the pilot failed to watch it continuously. It is true that some of the English pilots who refused to take their opinions of aircraft ready-made from the Royal Aircraft Factory, began to doubt the extraordinary virtues of a dihedral angle.

They even began to say that, by emphasizing automatic stability, a pronounced dihedral might reduce the powers of manœuvre. They said, furthermore, that what a fighting pilot wanted was not an aeroplane which flew itself, but one which he could fly. The much canvassed ideal of stability, with the backing of the Royal Aircraft Factory, had resulted in almost every British designed single-seater fighter used in the Royal Flying Corps having a dihedral angle. The flat top plane of the Camel was regarded as a rather daring experiment. And when the Camel exhibited such marked powers of manœuvre, it was attributed to that flat top plane. Conversely the S.E.5 was said to lack powers of quick manœuvre on account of the pronounced dihedral angle on both planes.

It is impossible to judge how much truth there was in these theories and counter-theories. Certainly they affected the regard pilots had for different aeroplanes, and when the present writer was given a Spad with Hispano-Suiza engine so that he might fly it from France to England, he expected it to be so sensitive as to be almost unmanageable and to exhibit every known vice. He was surprised and pleased when he discovered that it was not only easy to fly, but that it certainly did possess excellent powers of

THE SPAD

manœuvre—powers of manœuvre which seemed to be greater **than** those of the S.E.5.

And the manner in which the machine flew was very different. It flew in a mechanical manner, if one may so express it, instead of sailing through the air like an S.E. It seemed to demand the attention of its pilot all the time, though by no means in the unhealthy manner that had been suggested by those who did not know it, instead of going along in its own sweet way. It *responded*. And it responded quickly and sympathetically.

Many Royal Flying Corps pilots got to know the Spad, for, like the French Nieuport, it eventually formed the equipment of Royal Flying Corps units—No. 23 Squadron being one of the selected— and it is interesting to note how that came about. Spads were originally ordered by the Admiralty, but in November, 1916, Sir Douglas Haig drew up a memorandum demanding twenty extra fighting squadrons, and at a subsequent Air Board meeting General Trenchard insisted that the Royal Flying Corps should obtain everything that the Navy could afford to hand over. In addition to four complete Royal Naval Air Service squadrons, the Admiralty agreed to hand over to the Royal Flying Corps sixty complete Spads from their contract of one hundred and twenty then in course of fulfilment. By a further agreement in February, 1917, the Royal Flying Corps were given the complete programme of naval Spads in exchange for all the Sopwith triplanes then on order for the Royal Flying Corps.

As for the French service, the Spad was the mainstay of its fighting strength, and it was with this machine, in one of its numerous forms, that the greatest French pilots achieved most of their successes. Guynemer, who has been called with justice the greatest of all fighting pilots, used the Spad, and it was he who tried the motor-cannon armament, a form of armament which has recently been attracting a good deal of attention in England, the United States of America and elsewhere.

Fonck and Nungesser also used the Spad. It was fitted with various different engines, beginning with the 150 h.p. Hispano-Suiza, but the flying qualities remained very much the same. The French, however, when they had achieved an improvement in the performance of one of their aircraft by some experimental change or the fitting of a new and higher-powered engine, did not wait until they could equip a whole squadron before putting the improved machine in service. They immediately handed over one of the first machines to be produced to one of their best pilots. Consequently, new and faster Spads were in service, while the older ones were still in use. The 300 h.p. Spad did 135 m.p.h.

A classic simplicity is to be noted in the Spad. It was a single-bay biplane, with the points of intersection of the cable bracing stayed to the upper and lower main spars by short struts, an arrangement which gave an impression of two-bay bracing. The pilot was seated just behind and below the top plane. Part of the centre section was cut away in order to give him as good an outlook as possible upwards and forwards. Behind his head was a fairing and the top of the fuselage was faired to a rounded section. The engine cowling was neatly arranged, and between the cylinder banks the Vickers gun was arranged. In June, 1917, a 200 h.p. Spad armed with two Vickers guns replaced the lower-powered machines. The Royal Flying Corps machines had the Aldis tube sight, and on the French machines various forms of ring sight were used. Owing to the bellied fuselage the Spad could not be arranged to take the Cooper bomb-rack, but a container was evolved by the workshops of No. 19 Squadron which was fitted inside the fuselage behind the pilot. This container held two 25 lb. Cooper bombs only, as since the tail plane of the Spad was not adjustable a greater weight disturbed the balance.

Long exhaust pipes, often with flattened ends, were used and the machine was fairly quiet. The undercarriage was formed of faired V-struts, cross-braced, with short hinged axles and rubber shock-absorbers. In the air the pilot had a pleasing impression of rigidity, and the single-bay wing cell did not appear to flex or vibrate in the slightest, no matter what manœuvres were being done.

Like the S.E., the Spad is rich in war-time associations. It reminds one of the great French fighting pilots and their independence and daring.

THE D.H.2

Field of view was in the ascendant when the D.H.2 single-seater scout was designed and it certainly arrived at the ultimate in unobstructed outlook in a forwards direction. The pilot, sitting out in front in as small a nacelle as could be contrived to accommodate him and a single Lewis gun, could watch the whole of the forward hemisphere of sky and could also look back and upwards and down and backwards to a certain extent.

Another point in the D.H.2 was the unobstructed field of fire. The gun was clear of airscrews and other obstructions and, as it was originally mounted, it could be both elevated and traversed. Later it was thought that the traversing movements were of little real value, and in consequence the gun was limited in movement to elevation. Even so it was well placed right out in front.

If the theory had been correct that the chief things in the fighting aeroplane were fields of fire and fields of view, the D.H.2 of 1915 would have been the finest fighting aeroplane ever produced and would, without doubt, have given rise to further developments along the same lines. But the theory was not correct, or it was only partially correct. It was found, as the war went on, that performance was of at least equal importance to fields of fire and of view.

Now the D.H.2 was a good performer; but it could not compete with some of the tractor single-seaters which appeared later. In fact the D.H.2 represented a preponderance of military over aerodynamic qualities. And it was found, in the air war, curiously enough, that victory went more often to the machine with a preponderance of aerodynamic qualities over military ones.

This was the air war within the air war; the contest between purely military qualities in the aeroplanes used and purely aerodynamic qualities. Often the two were mutually hostile. Usually the air staff leant towards the military qualities; usually the fighting pilots leant towards the aerodynamic qualities. The fighting pilots wanted first of all a good aeroplane, and secondarily a gun and observation platform. The air staff wanted first a good gun and observation platform and secondarily an aeroplane.

H

THE D.H.2

Although the D.H.2 represented what was eventually found to be the wrong approach to the problem of producing a good fighting aeroplane, it was a bold and an ingenious attempt and it did do fine work on the Western Front. Indeed, for a time it looked as if the D.H.2 had found the real solution to the problem of the single-seater fighter, and that it would be developed in the future along the same general formula. But the Sopwith Pup appeared with a little more performance, able to hold height better and to get higher in less time.

And although the Sopwith Pup pilots had a relatively limited forward view, and although their single Vickers guns had to be supplied with interrupter gears to permit them to be fired through the field swept by the airscrew, they were generally considered to be superior as fighting machines.

The flying qualities of the D.H.2 were those of the pusher scout and were strikingly different from those of almost any other type of aeroplane. The D.H.2 was strongly one-sided. The rudder had to be held hard over against the effects of engine torque, and when the machine was being brought down prior to landing, the " blipping " of the engine on the thumb-switch was accompanied by a marked lurch to the side. The fitting of four-bladed propellers slightly reduced this effect.

A person used to a more evenly balanced machine, when he first went on to a D.H.2, found it exceedingly one-sided. Yet directly one got used to it it exercised a real and individual fascination. The pilot's position right out in front was in many ways extraordinarily pleasant. There were no engine fumes, and the ability to see where one was going ministered to the sensation of freedom. The present writer flew three different types of single-seater pusher aeroplane—the D.H.2, the F.E.8 and a Vickers single-seater pusher which did not come into production.

All of them had a similarity in handling qualities ; but probably the pleasantest was the D.H.2. It was with this machine that No. 24 Squadron, the first single-seater fighter squadron to go to France, was equipped. Later, No. 32 Squadron was also equipped with D.H.2s. The pilots of these squadrons discovered the handling qualities of the D.H.2, and found that it was capable of aerobatics and could be thrown about the sky with great ease and swiftness.

One of the favourite manœuvres, and one which was extensively used in combat was the Immelmann turn. This name seems to be no longer used ; yet I have not heard of any adequate substitute for it. For the true Immelmann turn is not a stalled turn. In a stalled turn the speed is allowed to fall off at the top of the upward curve and at the time when the machine is being tipped over into the turn itself, so that the first part of the subsequent down swoop is—partly, at any rate—the " fall " which follows a stall. But in the Immelmann turn in its true form, as I conceive it, and as it was generally accepted to be by those who practised it, the aeroplane is not stalled and has all the way round a margin of speed above its stalling speed.

The aeroplane, after first acquiring a high speed in relation to its performance, is pulled up on a zoom, and as it approaches the top of the zoom, but still before stalling point is reached, it is tipped over and to the side. The wings may and frequently do go well over the vertical at this point. The aeroplane, still being flown all the time and never stalled, is then brought round and down so that it pulls out of the subsequent dive facing in the opposite direction.

Captain Long, who achieved a long list of successes with the D.H.2, favoured this manœuvre and there were other pilots who used it to good effect. In their hands the D.H.2 became one of the chief instruments for overcoming the Fokker menace. The Fokkers had been creating havoc among the B.Es. and it was not until the D.H2s came out that their supremacy was seriously challenged.

Besides the Immelmann turn, several other less useful though more spectacular stunts were tried with the D.H.2. One pilot used the good forward outlook of the machine to do a sort of low switchback over the countryside with devastating effect on onlookers. Another specialized in the " cut " engine hoax which was as effective with a D.H.2 as it could possibly be. He would take off and at the moment of passing over the sheds or at some other moment when engine failure would have been peculiarly awkward, he would suddenly cut out the engine on the thumb switch meanwhile holding the aeroplane at its climbing angle. At the same time he would let out a heartrending shriek which carried to spectators on the ground and achieved the supreme purpose of a large number of Royal Flying Corps pilots—that of nearly giving them heart failure.

The engine of the D.H.2 was the 100 h.p. Monosoupape Gnôme and with this the maximum speed at 6,500 ft. was 86 m.p.h. The aeroplane climbed to 10,000 ft. in 25 minutes. A two-bay biplane of normal wood, fabric and wire construction, the D.H.2 had the tail booms converging at the rudder post in contrast to the F.E.8 which had them converging at the main spar of the tail plane.

A small windscreen was set in front of the pilot and the Lewis gun ammunition drums were carried in pockets at the sides of the nacelle. One additional point about the D.H.2 will be remembered by those who had much to do with it ; I refer to airscrew swinging, or " prop swinging " as it was called.

The mechanic climbed in under the tail booms and then stood before an engine and airscrew well within reach, much nearer the ground than in the average tractor and therefore more amenable to man-handling. In consequence, mechanics of the D.H.2 squadrons performed like virtuosos on the props. The Monosoupape was started after the command " switch off ; petrol on." The mechanic would then twist the rotary engine until an open exhaust valve was down and wait until petrol began to trickle out of the cylinder. He would then ask for the petrol to be turned off and would churn the engine backwards to form an appropriate petrol-air mixture.

The Monosoupape, with its enormous exhaust valve arc, was easy to swing and when they were turning it some of the mechanics would grab an airscrew blade in one hand and spin the engine continuously like a top. Then the " contact " order would be given and the engine would be swung in the right direction for starting. Again a continuously spinning motion would be imparted to it by an expert and energetic mechanic until it spluttered into life.

It was a pleasure to watch someone who knew how to handle a Monosoupape standing up to it within the tail booms of a D.H.2 and playing tunes on the engine. It is the memory which fixes this aeroplane most firmly in my mind.

THE D.H.5

This aeroplane could dive. That might be written in memory of the D.H.5. It may have been because of its backward stagger or for some other aerodynamic reason, or it may have been for some optical reason ; but it is certain that the sight of a formation of D.H.5s going down on an enemy formation was one of the most impressive things of the air war. They appeared to stand vertically on their noses and to fall out of the sky like a flight of bombs.

It was not, however, with the object of providing it with good diving qualities that the D.H.5 was designed. It was chiefly with the object of providing the pilot with the " perfect " fighting outlook yet at the same time giving him the advantages of tractor design. When the D.H.2 and F.E.8 were designed no efficient form of interrupter gear for guns existed, so these machines were made with the object of providing an unobstructed outlook in a forwards direction ; but they did so at the expense of what was believed to be the superior aerodynamic efficiency inherent in the tractor arrangement. With the introduction of the interrupter gear tractor fighters became possible—hence the Sopwith Pup and the D.H.5.

In designing the D.H.5 Captain de Havilland exercised his genius by retaining the unobstructed outlook and grafting it upon the tractor design. The pilot was seated out in front, immediately behind the engine. Below him, meeting the base of the fuselage, was the front spar of the lower plane. The upper plane, owing to the pronounced backward stagger, was well behind his head. If he sat in the cockpit and looked round he could see clearly upwards and forwards and downwards and to either side. The engine cowling restricted to some extent his view immediately in front and downwards. Upwards the view was also unrestricted in front, but the top plane limited it to the rear.

The armament was a single Vickers gun fixed to fire forwards in the line of flight through the field swept by the airscrew. Both Aldis tube and ring sights were provided. The fuselage was of normal wooden construction with rounded fairing on top. The engine was a 110 h.p. Le Rhône rotary. The maximum speed at 10,000 ft. was 102 m.p.h. and at 15,000 ft. it was 89 m.p.h.

In July, 1917, D.H.5 aeroplanes were sent to France, and during

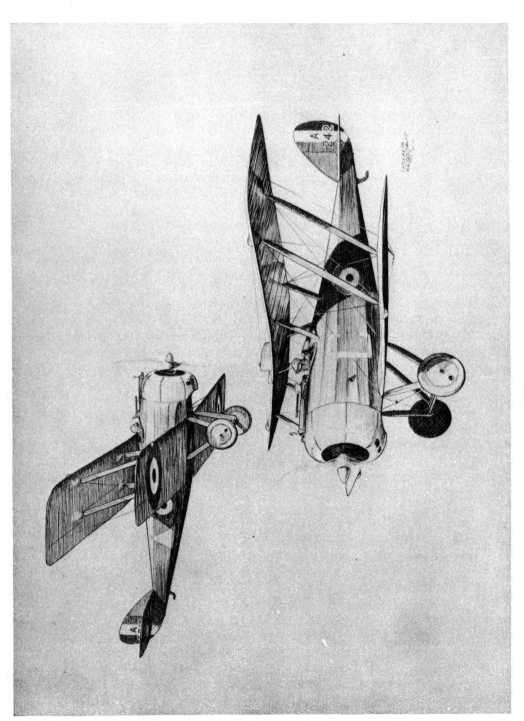

THE D.H.5

the early part of their use they were frequently on escort duty, escorting F.E.2bs on photographic and other patrols. Sometimes they co-operated with the Sopwith Pups, and the pilots of the two types soon found that the Pup, although an earlier introduction than the D.H.5, and although fitted with a lower-powered engine, was able to hold its height better when working near its ceiling. Consequently the Pups usually took the higher layers of the formation and the D.H.5s the lower layers.

Few aeroplanes have been subjected to so much adverse criticism among pilots as the D.H.5. A good many accidents happened when pilots were being trained to fly this machine, and it acquired the reputation of " losing " its elevator control if the gliding speed were allowed to fall to anything closely approaching the landing speed of about 50 m.p.h. Partly, perhaps, on this account it was never used extensively for low aerobatics. Pilots made it do all the normal aerobatics, but it was not chosen for advanced developments like the Camel.

Later on during the period it was on active service the D.H.5 was employed for low-flying attacks by British and Australian fighter squadrons, and it was thought that, for this purpose, the unobstructed outlook would be particularly useful. A formation of D.H.5s seen in the distance looked exactly like a flock or bevy— or whatever the correct term is—of tadpoles swimming. The fuselage shape, with its rather deep front and slim tail was a characteristic which impressed itself on the eye of the distant observer more than the backward stagger.

But the D.H.5 is a machine of especial importance to the student of the development of fighting aeroplanes, because it represented perhaps the most ingenious attempt to compromise between unobstructed outlook and aerodynamic efficiency. With the Sopwith Dolphin the D.H.5 strove to give the aerodynamic advantages of the tractor, with the outlook advantages of the pusher. After these machines designers in general accepted it as inevitable that outlook had, to some extent, to be sacrificed in order to get performance and the trend went towards the normal tractor aeroplane with such modifications as were possible to reduce the extent of the arcs of forward view blanked out by wings and fuselage.

Pusher types had been tried and had achieved a measure of success with their wide fields of fire and their unobstructed outlook. But as time went on and as fighting pilots made their needs felt with greater clarity, it became evident that performance came first in aerial combat, and that most pilots would be ready to sacrifice a certain amount of view if, in exchange, they could be given some extra performance. Had the D.H.5 shown better performance and handling qualities, it might yet have set a fashion in fighter types which would have prevailed for some time. But it did not show up as well as more straightforward tractor designs, and so it gave way to such higher-performance machines as the Camel, the S.E.5 and the Snipe.

THE D.H.4

The D.H.4 was the aeroplane whose coming was heralded by perhaps the most remarkable series of rumours that were ever current in that place of rumours, the Royal Flying Corps. In speed and climb the D.H.4 was said to be something so far ahead of any previous machine that the Allied forces would be able to achieve an air superiority unquestioned and unquestionable. And in actual fact the D.H.4 was a fine aeroplane with a good performance, and it did contribute to our air superiority in the last year of the War.

Originally it had a 240 h.p. B.H.P. engine, but a later version had the Rolls-Royce Eagle engine of 375 h.p. With the latter engine the top speed at 6,500 ft. was 136·5 m.p.h., while at 15,000 ft. the top speed was 126 m.p.h. The aeroplane could climb to 10,000 ft. in 9 minutes and to 15,000 ft. in 16½ minutes. The ceiling was 22,000 ft., and that ceiling was one of the things which made the D.H.4 seem so desirable to bombing pilots when it was first heard about in the squadrons. For it was generally held that an aeroplane flying at 20,000 ft. was virtually safe from anti-aircraft fire, and bomber pilots looked forward with longing to the machine that would enable them to do their long raids out of range of the guns.

In addition, it was held that very few single-seater fighters would be able to reach the D.H.4 if it went over the lines near its ceiling and stayed high for the whole outward passage. For the homeward journey there was that turn of speed which would enable it to get away from enemy fighters. Actuality, as always happens, fell short of expectation and the D.H.4, when it did at last appear in the squadrons in quantity, did not have so marked a superiority in height and speed as to make it invulnerable or unattackable. On the contrary, it often had to fight its way to and from its objectives.

Reference should be made to the commentary dealing with the D.H.9 wherein the development of this type of machine is traced from the D.H.4. But the things to be noted in this picture are the forward firing Vickers gun, the two bombs on the rack underneath the fuselage, the radiator shutters, the Scarff mounting

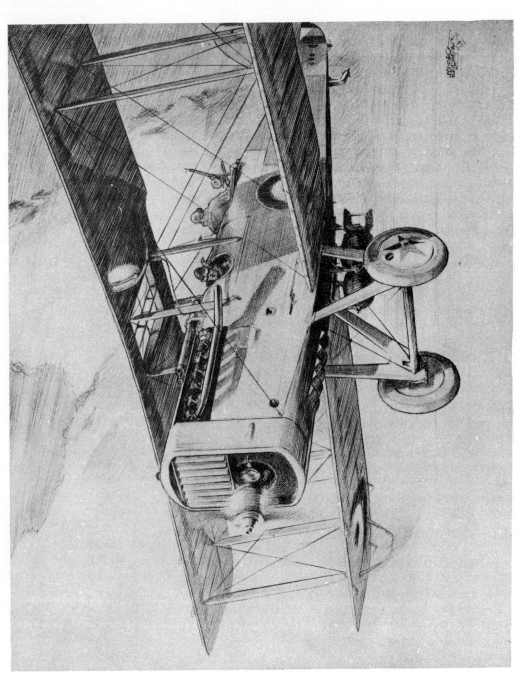

THE D.H.4

for the observer's Lewis gun, and the " window " in the centre section for improving the pilot's outlook.

It will also be observed that there is a considerable distance between the pilot and the observer. This, at the time, was criticized on the grounds that it would impair co-operation between them and would prevent the aeroplane being fought as effectively as possible. On the other hand it is to be noted that the pilot enjoys a view downward and forward at a steep angle and that this steep angle is secured by virtue of his position well forward.

The D.H.4 was used in the Royal Flying Corps, the Royal Naval Air Service, the Independent Air Force and the Royal Air Force. Long-range bombing was its principal duty, and it was one of the type with which the technique of formation flying and fighting was developed to the fullest extent. The machine was usually fitted with a four-bladed airscrew, and the colouring of these machines was usually a hue between dull khaki and dark green. The D.H.4s used in Mesopotamia were light khaki. The undersurfaces were cream coloured, with grey engine cowling and grey fuselage as far back as the observer's cockpit. The radiator shutters sometimes bore squadron colourings.

An interesting constructional feature of the D.H.4 and its successors, the D.H.9 and D.H.9a, was the free use of plywood in the fuselage structure. The fuselage from the nose to a point just aft of the observer's cockpit was covered with a plywood skin, and even the engine-bearers were supported by transverse frames having as many as a dozen or more plies of thin wood glued together. With this form of construction it was claimed that it was possible to riddle the front end of the fuselage with bullets without impairing the strength of the structure, whereas by using the more customary construction with wire bracing and a multiplicity of small metal fittings, a single lucky shot might do serious structural damage.

THE D.H.9

One of the most widely used bombing aeroplanes in the Royal Flying Corps was the D.H.9. This was a development of the D.H.4 adapted to take the mass-produced Puma engine. But although the dimensions were much the same, the first glance at the illustration of this machine will reveal that its appearance differed markedly from the earlier type. The entire rearrangement of the nose and engine cowling and the altered position of the pilot, with the cockpit back behind the top plane instead of under the centre-section, combine to change entirely the silhouette.

Nor did the D.H.9 ever enjoy the great reputation of the D.H.4. The D.H.4 came to France and was received there as a sort of wonder aeroplane with an incredible ceiling and, for a machine of that type, an incredible top speed. The D.H.9 was looked upon as a D.H.4 " spoilt " by official interference. The altered pilot's position was regarded by many pilots as giving an academic advantage, by enabling pilot and observer to be in touch with one another and by improving the pilot's outlook, while it sacrificed the practical advantage of good performance. This change of position of the pilot's seat was, perhaps, largely made for safety's sake, as it relieved the pilot from being in an unenviable position between the engine and the petrol tanks, and at the same time gave the observer a chance of getting the machine down safely if the pilot was put out of action. However, this change did sacrifice good performance, and pilots had a grudge against it for this reason.

Yet it happened that this aeroplane, which was so little admired compared with other types, had to do an enormous amount of hard work during the War. It was the key machine for the Independent Air Force operations which included long-distance raids on enemy positions. It had to go out to attack the Rhine towns, and consequently it may be said to have instituted the method of strategical bombing so far as the Allies were concerned. Moreover, when once it had got going the D.H.9 stayed in the service for a very long period. It was fitted with various engines, sometimes with a change of name and sometimes without, but always with the object of improving its performance. But none of the standardized engines seemed to give it the speed and climb that

THE D.H.9

were always being promised, and it was always some 25 m.p.h. behind the D.H.4.

It was only when a Napier Lion was fitted that it showed really advanced performance. When the first machine so fitted was at Martlesham Heath, the aircraft and armament experimental station, two of the officers there noted its qualities and decided to demonstrate them. So they made an observed climb to absolute ceiling. The height reached was 30,500 ft., and they took $66\frac{1}{4}$ minutes to get there. At the time it was an international aeroplane height record, and so it was hailed in the Press.

For the two officers the reward, instead of being a laurel wreath and a telegram of congratulation from the Chief of the Air Staff, was a period of open arrest for having disobeyed some rule or regulation, I forget which one. It is to be presumed that the authorities took this action *pour encourager les autres*. At any rate, since then Great Britain, although conspicuously backward in the obtaining of world's air records in mass, has done some highly successful high flights, including those by Squadron Leader F. R. D. Swain and Flight Lieutenant M. J. Adam.

With full war load the Napier D.H. could get to 24,000 ft. in 53 minutes, and the full load included two 112 lb. bombs, ammunition and two machine guns. At 24,000 ft. its speed was 95 m.p.h. But it must be repeated that, in this high performance form, the D.H.9 did not see active service. During the time it was in use in France, in Palestine and the Adriatic, and for submarine patrol off the East Coast of England, it was a poor performer and casualties on the long-distance bombing raids were high. With the 230 h.p. B.H.P. engine the speed was 115 m.p.h. at 10,000 ft. At this height, with the Napier Lion engine, the speed was 140 m.p.h. The span was 42 ft. $4\frac{1}{2}$ in., the length 30 ft. 10 in., and the height 11 ft. 2 in. The weight empty was 2,225 lb. and loaded 3,300 lb.

It is worth noting, in the picture, the marked dihedral angle and the characteristic D.H. tail with a fin and rudder shape which, with slight variations, was to persist through a whole series of civil machines and eventually to find an echo in the famous Moth. It will be noticed, too, that the observer's gun mounting is of the Scarff type. This was a rotatable ring with a hinged and balanced arm on which the Lewis gun was mounted. This enabled the gunner to swing the gun quickly and to obtain the full field of fire allowed by the structure of the aeroplane. He could fire almost vertically downwards beside the fuselage, and he could fire vertically upwards by swinging up the arm and swivelling the gun. Later on twin Lewis guns were fitted to the observer's mounting.

Another point to be noted is the radiator position. This was unusual at the time, when the car idea prevailed, and most radiators were around the airscrew shaft as in the S.E.5 and the Spad. The positioning of the radiator underneath the fuselage led eventually to the use of the retractable radiator which enjoyed a vogue reaching to 1937. The pilot was furnished with a fixed Vickers gun firing forwards through the field swept by the airscrew.

Production rates with the D.H.9 were high by the time the armistice was signed, and they were being turned out at a rate approaching that at which mass-produced motor-cars are produced. In consequence the Royal Air Force took a long time to get rid of its last D.H.9. Indeed this type of machine showed a tenacity to life which might have been more admired had it also shown more outstanding performance qualities. Thirteen squadrons were equipped with the D.H.9, and it was used for a very large number of odd duties, including experimental work.

When going on bomb raids the D.H.9 carried its bombs in racks under the wings. Pilots found that their only hope of returning lay in maintaining formation. They did not adopt, however, the close kind of formation that is now seen at the Hendon Royal Air Force Display, but a much looser grouping which permitted each individual machine a certain amount of freedom of manœuvre. When flying in this manner it was found that well-trained observers could do a great deal with their Lewis guns to stave off attacks by single-seater fighters.

After the War the D.H.9 took on a homely sort of quality. It was well liked, although it never seemed to arouse the enthusiasm which the less staid aeroplanes aroused. So if all the D.H.9 qualities are put together, and if it is sought to point out one outstanding one, it must be the quality of series production. The D.H.9 was the machine which was selected for the War's biggest attempt at Fordism in airframe production. It was pre-eminently the mass-produced aeroplane.

I have mentioned two engines with which it was fitted, but there were others. One was the Fiat, which emphasized still further the comfort characteristics of the D.H.9, for it was a sweet-running engine. Then there was the Liberty, but with that the machine became the D.H.9a which I deal with elsewhere.

The machine depicted by Leonard Bridgman is one of those which belonged to No. 144 Squadron, one of the thirteen units which were equipped with this aeroplane.

THE D.H.9A

Strategical bombing was initiated so far as the British flying services were concerned with the D.H.9a, for this was the machine largely used by the Independent Air Force for air raids on German towns. It comes in the direct line of descent from the D.H.9, and the commentary which deals with this machine provides a suitable introduction to the D.H.9a. In addition, Leonard Bridgman's picture of the D.H.9 shows at first glance the outstanding difference which made these two types look so far removed from one another when they were seen in the air.

The D.H.9 nose is of the pointed sort with the underneath radiator, whereas the D.H.9a has a massive square nose with the radiator in what may be called " car position " with the airscrew shaft protruding through a hole. The D.H.9a, therefore, looked more like the original D.H.4, but pilot and observer were arranged close together.

With the Liberty engine of 400 h.p., about whose design and development something is said in the commentary on the D.H.9, the D.H.9a weighed 4,815 lb. when fully loaded and 2,656 lb. when empty. The wing loading per square foot was 9·89 lb. which, for the time, was on the high side. The aeroplane could climb to 10,000 ft. in 15·8 minutes and to 15,000 ft. in 33 minutes, and its speed at 10,000 ft. was 114 m.p.h. and at 15,000 ft. 106 m.p.h.

It has been said that strategical bombing was initiated by these machines, and it may be worth noting that this is a form of aerial attack which has been strongly advocated in recent years by the specialists. It consists in attacking the enemy at points of military importance far behind his own lines. It aims at crippling the sources of supply as quickly as possible. It is a method which was originated by the Germans and which has since been judged as having been of real value to them during the War.

Their strategical bomb raids, which the Independent Air Force sought to imitate, diverted many fighting aeroplanes and large numbers of guns and gun crews from the battle zone in France. The German raids have been adversely criticized on the grounds that they killed and wounded large numbers of civilians and of women and children, but it may be that that killing and wounding was accidental. Indeed, it could be regarded as the fault of the

THE D.H.9A

British authorities for housing women and children and civilians close to points of military importance such as docks, centres of government, and munitions and aircraft factories.

At any rate, it appears that strategical bombing will be a recognized and important part of any future war in the air, and consequently the D.H.9a, which was the first aeroplane which may be said to have been specifically planned for that purpose, possesses historical interest. It was designed on the theory that for daylight raids a high performance was the best protection against attack by opposing fighters. The bomb load was relatively small, and the armament consisted of a single Vickers gun firing through the field swept by the airscrew by means of interrupter gear, and a pair of Lewis guns on a Scarff mounting used by the observer.

The Independent Air Force found, however, that the performance of these machines was not in fact adequate protection for them. They suffered severe losses, and in order to protect themselves they developed the technique of making their bombing raids in formation and exercising a degree of fire control in order to concentrate fire upon any single-seater which seemed to menace their safety.

In construction the D.H.9a followed the D.H.9. It was built mainly of ash and spruce. The fuselage was formed of four longerons, braced with tie-rods and struts, and covered partly with plywood and partly with fabric. The wings were of the two-spar type with compression and former ribs, covered in doped fabric. The interplane struts were of streamline section, and swaged flying and landing wires and undercarriage bracing wires were used. There were also on each side of the fuselage a pair of anti-drag wires from the lower part of the nose of the fuselage back to the inner interplane strut sockets.

Structurally and in design the D.H.9a cannot be regarded as remarkable, for it followed on the line which had already been clearly defined by previous types. But strategically it has importance in that it was the instrument of a strategical method which has since grown enormously in importance and which, in the opinion of some authorities, might become a major factor in determining the course of any future war.

The Liberty was a proper consort for the D.H.9, for it also was the war's biggest attempt at Fordism in aero-engine production. The Liberty version became the D.H.9a and this machine, which is illustrated by Leonard Bridgman in another picture, was slightly bigger in every way than the original D.H.9. The stories current about the way in which the Liberty was designed, which travelled the round of the Royal Flying Corps and Royal Naval Air Service messes, had a distinctly transatlantic flavour.

It was said that half a dozen or a dozen or a score—I forget the details—of America's leading engineers were closeted in a locked room under a vow not to come out until they had devised the world's finest aircraft engine and an engine, moreover, capable of mass production on a huge scale. When this story first went about— like so many American stories—it was listened to with awe and approval. America was coming into the air war with characteristic American enterprise. When the story was repeated after British pilots had had some experience of the Liberty engine in the air, it was looked upon as the cream of satire. For the truth is that, whether the engine really had its origin in the way related or not, the result was disappointing.

British pilots were not very favourably disposed towards coil ignition, and the Liberty was the first aero engine to introduce this in a big way into the flying service. Then the Liberty coil ignition did not work very well at first. There were engine failures and forced landings. The story about the closeted American engineers was gradually converted into an enormous joke, to be related with satiric emphasis at every fresh dereliction of the Liberty motor. Nevertheless, it must be confessed that when the Liberty was finally persuaded to go well, it went very well.

AVRO 504K

Here it is, the inevitable Avro 504k. For years no air meeting, no aerodrome, no air race, no pageant or display, was complete without an Avro 504k. Everybody knew it, everybody flew it. It was used for every known aerial activity, including touring, aerobatics, instruction, bombing, photography, joy-riding, racing and banner-towing. I saw an Avro 504 in 1913, in the Aerial Derby, and I saw one again on the day I wrote these words, twenty-four years afterwards, struggling across the sky with an advertisement banner tugging behind it.

Of course the Avro has gone through many modifications since it first appeared ; but it is still recognizably and fundamentally the same aeroplane to-day as it was then. It is the most remarkable example of longevity in the history of aeronautics. The number of miles which must have been flown by Avro 504's or their descendants, must be astronomical. The number of pilots who have been instructed in them or who have used them for one purpose or another, must be œcumenical.

Its store of vitality lay, without doubt, in its classical simplicity of conception, and its classical harmony of shape. There was nothing unnecessary about it and the areas of the control and lifting components were harmoniously related to one another. It was a thing which came together like a work of art comes together, by a sudden inexplicable harmoniousness of parts. It is the supreme example of the aeroplane as the work of art and the illustration of the truth of what I said in the Preface about the change that has come about in design methods. The Avro 504k was the antithesis of the aeroplane assembled from pieces of elaborately acquired and carefully tested information gathered together in different places. It was not the outcome of numerous researches conducted in all kinds of places and by all kinds of people. There was no synthesis of contributions from specialists.

On the contrary, Sir Alliott Verdon Roe achieved in the old Avro one of those works of genius whose essential quality is that they spring complete from their creator's brain. People constantly speak of books, plays, paintings and pieces of music that will " live." If one of these works will " live," it is paid the supreme compliment. On that basis of judgment, the Avro must be accepted as a

THE AVRO 504K

really " great " aeroplane. For, so far as aeronautical machinery is concerned, it proved its capacity to " live."

It was in the Aerial Derby of 1913 that the Avro 504 first burst upon the world, for although this tractor biplane was not given that series number and although the first machine to bear that number did not appear until a little later in the same year, the machine that took part in the Aerial Derby was the precursor of the 504 series. As Mr. R. Dallas Brett writes of it in his " History of British Aviation " : " This wonderful machine has developed solely by means of detailed refinements into the Avro Tutor of to-day. In essentials the general layout is the same. If the identical biplane which Raynham flew in the Aerial Derby on September 20th, 1913, could land at Heston or Hanworth to-morrow its appearance would excite little comment ; for it would not be conspicuously old-fashioned. Avros of the 504 type have flown millions of miles in the hands of ' joy-ride ' concerns and more people have had their first flights in them than in any other type. Their freedom from vices in the air, the ease with which they can be flown in and out of small fields which would be dangerous for ordinary light aeroplanes and their ability to perform many kinds of aerobatics have made them immensely popular with pilots all over the world. With the possible exception of the de Havilland Moth, the Avro 504 in its various stages of development, can claim to have proved the most successful aeroplane, judged by the number sold, that has ever been produced."

Raynham finished fourth in that Aerial Derby of 1913, which was a fine race and was won by Gustav Hamel in a Morane-Saulnier monoplane. Raynham's speed for the race was 66·5 m.p.h. The engine of his Avro was an 80 h.p. Gnôme. In November of the same year, Raynham took the first true Avro 504—for, as I have said, the machine in the Aerial Derby was not strictly speaking a 504 although it was the parent of the type—to Farnborough for government performance trials. And here we have the first indication of the qualities of this remarkable aeroplane. Before quoting the figures I must emphasize that the date is November, 1913.

With one passenger and fuel for three hours' flight, the Avro achieved a maximum speed of 80·9 m.p.h. Its stalling speed was 43 m.p.h. and it could climb to 1,000 ft. in 1 minute 45 seconds. When war broke out in 1914 the Avro 504 was, with one exception, the fastest two-seater aeroplane available to the Service. It was a medium sized machine for its time, with a wing span of 36 ft. and a length of about 29 ft.

I

With the 110 h.p. Le Rhône engine its performance was good, the top speed being over 90 m.p.h. and the climb to 10,000 ft. taking only sixteen minutes. Can I recall for those thousands who got to know the Avro intimately something of this machine's personality ? My own impression when I got into one for the first time, was of the large size of the fuselage. After things like Maurice Farmans the Avro fuselage seemed very roomy. Then there was that wooden control stick with the thumb switch as a button on top of it and the doped fabric sides of the fuselage which were almost transparent. There was, of course, the smell of castor oil. My own experience of the Avro began with the 80 h.p. Gnôme engine, but I later flew it with other engines.

In the air there was that balanced rudder. Pupils looked upon it with respect. It was said to be " terrifically powerful," and that one had to use the rudder very carefully indeed or the aeroplane tried to come round and bite one. When being instructed in an Avro in the early days of the War, the pupil sat in the front seat, with the engine in his lap and oil and petrol a good deal too much in evidence for anything that remained of his peace of mind. There were no instruments and the instructor in the rear seat had the switches.

There were no speaking tubes or means of verbal communication between pupil and instructor, and consequently the method employed was that of giving the stick or the rudder bar a jab in the right direction when the pupil tended to move one of them in the wrong direction. *Ab initio* training was not done with these machines in the early War period, for they were regarded as advanced training machines. And there is no doubt that they did inculcate the true principles of good flying in a way few other machines could have done so well.

Gradually the Avro passed from the time when it was treated with respect, to the time when it was treated with disrespect. And it is during this latter period that an aeroplane really shows its qualities. While pilots are handling it with velvet gloves, an aeroplane does not need any superlative qualities of control or stability if it is to get through its flying without mishap. But when pilots start to throw the machine about and to see what can be done with it, the call on the qualities of control and stability becomes greater. The aeroplanes which pass through the period of disrespectful flying successfully have passed through a very stiff examination.

The Avro passed through this period with complete success. The more the pilots demanded from it, the more it gave. There seemed no end to its fund of responses. It saved bad pilots from the effects of their mistakes and it enabled good pilots to reap the full benefits from their skill. And all the time the demands upon it grew. Perhaps the severest demand of all came when the Avro 504k went into service at the Smith-Barry School of Special Flying at Gosport.

Royal Air Force authorities do not like to hear it said to-day, but I am going to risk their displeasure by saying that the Gosport system is the foundation of all good flying training and remains the foundation of all good flying training to-day. Flying methods have changed enormously. With the coming of the tricycle undercarriage they may change yet more. For example, there is the method of approach. It is no longer a crime of the first magnitude to rumble in with the engine; in fact, commercial pilots are in some cases taught to approach in that manner. But the method taught at Gosport did not tolerate such concessions to the weaknesses of visual judgment. There it was necessary to judge every inch of the approach and to bring the machine into the right position for the landing without having recourse to the engine. Pilots landed on the tarmac and on at least one occasion a Gosport pilot landed so that the aeroplane finished its landing run inside the shed! And remember those machines had no wheel brakes.

Then again the impossible was constantly being converted not only into the possible but into the essential. Pilots were taught to take off and land in all kinds of unorthodox ways—ways which brought gasps of astonishment from those who had been taught the previously popular fly-by-rote methods. They were taught, or at any rate allowed, to spin as low as possible. And all this was being done with the Avro 504k. Leonard Bridgman depicts the Avro 504k with Monosoupape engine bearing the triangle marking of the Smith-Barry School of Special Flying in the sort of attitude which was popular among those who went through the course. A Gosport instructor was one who could not be put out, literally or figuratively, no matter what position his machine was in and who could put it down and take it off again as near the limits of the aeroplane's capabilities as possible.

To see these pilots demonstrating was to realize not only the high degree of skill developed by the system, but also the high degree of controllability of the Avro 504k aeroplane. The system was brilliantly conceived, but so was the aeroplane which made it possible. So, the Avro 504k shares with Colonel Smith-Barry, Captain Duncan Bell-Irving and his staff, the honour of having instituted and brought to perfection what remains to-day the finest school of advanced flying training there has ever been.

Nor must it be forgotten that the Avro was used as a bomber, against the Friedrichschaten sheds, as a fighter, and as a seaplane. Among service types there have been many examples, which are described in this volume, of machines which remained in use for long periods ; but the Avro permeated civil as well as service flying. By the end of the War, 10,000 of them had been made. It was to be found everywhere. Consequently, if one could sift, from the memories of those who have been closely in touch with aviation since it began until to-day, the shapes of aeroplanes that have gone before, one would find that the dominant one would be the Avro 504k.

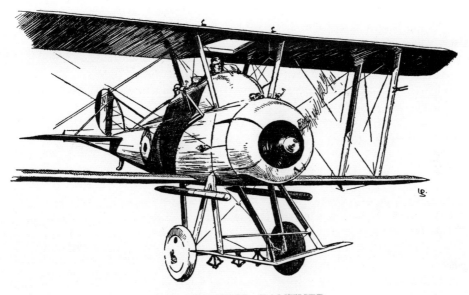

THE PARNALL PANTHER
First Deck-landing Machine

THE HAMBLE BABY

The truth in aviation of the saying that there is nothing new under the sun is illustrated again and again in these pages. Those features and components which are so highly regarded to-day as being " latest developments " were one and all thought of and tried years and years ago. That they did not come into use was frequently the result of an insufficiently advanced constructional technique to cope with the practical problems.

Here, in the Hamble Baby, we have proof of the fact that, in aviation, there is nothing new under the sun. For a component of the latest aeroplanes which is invariably referred to as if it were a recent development was tried thoroughly in the Hamble Baby more than twenty years ago. It was the wing flap.

Wing flaps increase speed range. They enable highly loaded aeroplanes to be brought down and landed slowly. They are really " variable camber " devices, and the use of that term will remind those who have followed aeronautical history from the beginning that even the Fairey flap gear was foreseen when people talked about the need for " variable camber " wings.

Squadron Leader Maurice Wright, who as Government test pilot at the Isle of Grain and elsewhere, flew in all some two hundred and eighty different types of aeroplanes and therefore set up a record which few people have beaten even now, did the tests with the Hamble Baby. The name Hamble came from the Hamble River, where the Fairey Company's seaplane base was situated. The engine of the Hamble Baby was the 130 h.p. Clergêt, and one of the reasons for the fitting of the flap gear was that it was desired that the machine should be capable of carrying a big load of bombs.

Originally the Sopwith Schneider seaplane, or Baby, the Hamble Baby had this special set of flapped wings. When as a seaplane it fell into disfavour with the Admiralty some Hamble Baby Converts were supplied with wheel undercarriages in place of the floats. The same set of " N " struts was used and longitudinal skids were substituted for the floats. The wheels on a long axle were slung across the skids and sprung with shock-absorber rope.

The Hamble Baby flap gear was also the ailerons. That is to say, the ailerons extended for the entire length of the wings. In

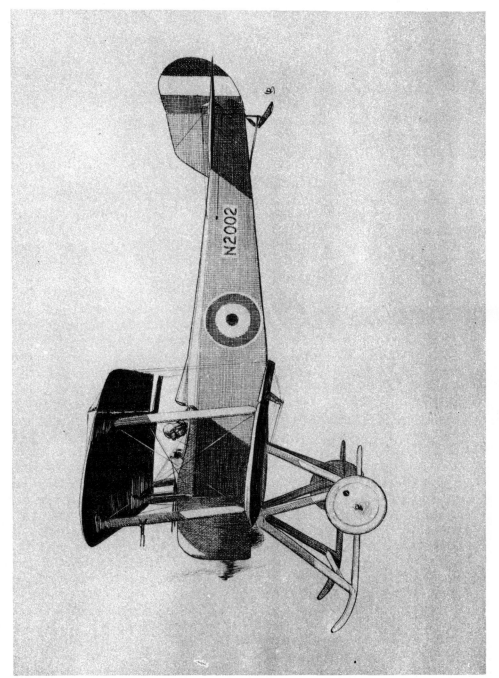

THE HAMBLE BABY CONVERT

consequence of this the controls were heavy, but they gave good results at low speeds right down to the stall. Wing flaps of various kinds were forgotten after the Hamble Baby had gone out of the picture ; but they were to be rediscovered by the Americans and to receive the homage due to new ideas at a considerable remove from the time they were actually first tried.

When historians of the future come to compile a complete picture of aeronautical development, they must include, if they are just, the Hamble Baby as being the aeroplane which, with the aid of the Fairey variable camber gear, showed the way to developments which were to enable much higher speeds to be reached in the future without additional risk and without additional flying difficulties.

THE NIEUPORT NIGHTHAWK

Aerobatic pilots found a machine which might have been made expressly for their benefit in the Nieuport Nighthawk. Fairly small, with a wing span of only 28 feet, rigid and with a good performance, the top speed being 145 m.p.h., and the climb to 20,000 ft. occupying only 22 minutes, the Nighthawk was one of Mr. H. P. Folland's designs, and it was capable of great rapidity of manœuvre and it possessed extraordinarily well-balanced controls.

It was a competitive design against Sopwith and four other firms, and in order that it should be comparable on a production basis with the other machines, it incorporated a number of S.E.5 parts. These included the fuselage fittings, rudder bar and stick controls, axle and wheels, the rear skid and a few other components. But although it used S.E. parts, it was far from being an S.E. In fact, it was totally unlike an S.E. to fly.

The outlook was good, with the pilot well placed close up behind the A.B.C. Dragonfly radial engine. And it was a feature of the machine that the weights were massed close together, a feature to which was attributed in some measure the aeroplane's quickness on the controls. The wing area was 270 sq. ft., and the weight of the aeroplane, when fully loaded, was 2,240 lb. This is an increase in wing area of 20 sq. ft. over the earlier S.E.5. The fuel tanks were shaped to complete the fuselage contours and were arranged alongside the pilot.

The Nieuport Nighthawk was used for making a number of trials with some special crash-proof tanks. These tanks were covered with rubber envelopes. They behaved perfectly until, one day, it was noticed that the Nighthawk seemed to have grown fatter. And the next day there was no doubt about it. Either the Nighthawk was getting that middle-aged spread or it was going to have a baby. Examination showed that petrol had seeped in between the tanks themselves and their rubber envelopes, and that warm weather had provided enough vapour pressure to swell out the tanks. Other work was done with these tanks, but they invariably exhibited, when they were built to Nighthawk shape, this tendency to obesity.

THE NIEUPORT NIGHTHAWK

In the air the Nieuport Nighthawk was a delight to handle. It did all the aerobatic manœuvres quickly and easily. It spun quickly, but was so controllable that it could be extricated by a mere touch. Its upside-down flying qualities were almost as good as its right-way-up flying qualities.

If one seeks to look at the Nighthawk from the historical angle, and to find its place in the scheme of things, one notes that it represented an intermediate stage between the small rotary-engined, highly manœuvrable machine and the much larger radial or V-engined machine. It was probably the last of the " quick " aeroplanes, and it gave way to those with higher translational speeds, perhaps, but with slower responses to control movements.

Some of the special aeroplanes which have been built for Continental aerobatic pilots since the War might have competed with the Nighthawk in point of manœuvre, but I doubt if any of them would have been much better than it was. It would have made an ideal aeroplane for aerobatics if an entirely trustworthy engine could have been found for it.

FLYCATCHERS

THE FAIREY FLYCATCHER

Better known to the general public than almost any other single-seater fighter—although not by name—the Fairey Flycatcher was for many years the aeroplane chosen to do the converging attack item at the Royal Air Force Display. This demonstration was done by pilots of the Fleet Air Arm, and it was done so well that it normally provided the best spectacle in the programme. It also showed the high degree of co-ordination between the pilots and the good powers of manœuvre of the aeroplanes.

Because the formation flying done with this machine was so skilful, it is appropriate that Leonard Bridgman should show a Fleet Fighter Flight, No. 405, in formation. Wing-tip to wing-tip, this is how the Flycatchers were first seen when they appeared in public. And their subsequent displays of formation tactics were always impressive and a strong testimony to the powers of control of the machines and to the good outlook enjoyed by the pilots.

There were many features of interest in the construction and general design of the Fairey Flycatcher. It could be used as a shipboard fighter, a landplane, a seaplane or an amphibian, and the normal engine was the 385 h.p. Armstrong Siddeley Jaguar. The top centre section was carried above the fuselage with one set of " N " steel tube struts on either side of the fuselage. The lower plane had no dihedral, but the upper one had a fairly marked dihedral. The wing structure was of wood, covered with doped fabric.

In the comments on the Hamble Baby something is said about the early work with wing flaps. The Flycatcher carried on that work, for it carried wing flaps on all four wings. The outer sections of these flaps acted as ailerons. The surfaces were not balanced, but the tail plane was adjustable. In landplane form the cross-axle type undercarriage had oleo legs. This wheel undercarriage was interchangeable with an ordinary float undercarriage or with an amphibian undercarriage.

Armament consisted of two Vickers guns mounted at the side of the fuselage. The weight of the Flycatcher, when fully loaded, was 3,028 lb., and the maximum speed at 5,000 ft. was 134 miles an hour. The machine took 8 minutes 38 seconds to climb to 10,000 ft. and the service ceiling was 20,600 ft. As a seaplane the maximum speed was 113 knots, and the climb to 10,000 ft. took fourteen minutes. In this form the service ceiling was brought down to 14,000 ft.

THE SIDDELEY SISKIN

Like Topsy, the Siskin " growed." It did not appear as a fully competent design to be taken up or discarded by the Royal Air Force. It started, tentatively, in one form ; it changed and merged into another form, and even after it had been adopted it went through further modifications.

Primarily the work of Major F. M. Green, the Siddeley Siskin was one of the first positively post-war single-seater fighters introduced into the Royal Air Force. The Snipe's period of use overlapped the War period, but the Siskin marked the passage from war to peace and also the introduction of a new conception of the fighting aeroplane.

The rotary engine had gone and the stationary radial had come in its place, though not without a severe struggle, during which many unsuccessful attempts had been made to introduce radial engines. Meanwhile, the liquid-cooled V engine had always marched alongside the air-cooled engine, as it still does, and the choice of the radial for the single-seater fighter was of special interest.

It happens that the Siddeley Siskin was the last Royal Air Force type tested by the present writer in his capacity as test pilot at Martlesham Heath, and it certainly seemed to represent a departure from previous single-seater fighters in more than one way. It appeared first of all as a wooden biplane, or sesquiplane, with a system of flying bracing which extended from the sockets of the steel interplane struts right to the undercarriage struts. The undercarriage itself was of the oleo type, with an enormously long leg travel, and the consequence was that the Siskin could be landed without the pilot himself being aware of the instant at which the wheels first touched the ground.

The engine was the A.B.C. Dragonfly, an engine which, although it never proved successful itself, led the way to the successful radial. The aeroplane was extremely easy to fly, and it is probable that it was, at the time it first appeared, the easiest single-seater fighter ever introduced into the flying service. In the past, single-seater fighters had been quick, snappy, short-tempered and sometimes vicious.

SISKINS

But the Siskin was gentle, easy-going, calm, good-tempered—
a marked contrast to previous machines and especially to such a
type as the B.A.T. Bantam, in whose performance trials the writer
had also been engaged. Taking off, the Siskin presented an
eminently ludicrous appearance, for its great oleo legs gradually
stretched as the wings took more and more of the weight and left
the wheels still running along the ground while the fuselage rose
higher and higher.

In the air the Siskin was amenable to discipline and would do
loops, rolls—both flick and slow—and spins graciously, if not very
quickly. The outlook was markedly good and the cockpit arrangements and flying qualities comfortable. But really the Siskin
waited on the engine. The A.B.C. held it back, and it was not
until the Armstrong Siddeley Jaguar proved itself that the machine
got into its stride and was ordered in quantity for the Royal Air
Force.

Thereafter it became a very popular machine with R.A.F. pilots,
and an enormous amount of formation flying was done with it.
It was also used for radio-telephony experiments and for racing.
No. 1 Squadron of the Royal Air Force was one of those to be
fully equipped with the Siddeley Siskin, and the flight of three
aeroplanes shown by Leonard Bridgman belong to this squadron.
The leader's strut and tail streamers are of the sleeve type, a form
which was adopted after the Siskin had come into service. It
was a sign of the increasing performance, for it was found that the
flat streamers used previously on struts and tail would not stand
up to the higher speeds.

There is one thing in this picture which seems to me to epitomize
the Siddeley Siskin. It is the small step on the underside of the
fuselage below the pilot's cockpit. The Siskin was, as I have said,
above all things a comfortable machine—a human machine, and
it ministered to the comfort and convenience of its pilot in more
ways than one. This step enabled him to climb to his seat without
trouble. Drag did not seem of much importance compared with
the pilot's convenience in getting in and out. Another thing to
be noted is that the engine at the time was uncowled. The
Siskin came in before the world's designers had applied the
schemes first mooted in such machines as the Sopwith Tabloid
and the Bristol Monoplane, before any genuine attempt had been
made to standardize a low drag form of cowling.

But later on the Townend ring was fitted to Siskin aeroplanes
with a consequent gain in speed. This ring was of aerofoil
section, and it completely surrounded the radial engine. Its
function was to control the air flow past the engine, and it did this

to such effect that there was a considerable reduction in drag and a consequent gain in speed.

Another of the changes through which the Siskin went was the fundamental one from wood construction to metal construction. But through all these stages the aeroplane retained its chief characteristics and was still recognizable as the machine which, if my memory is correct, had come to Martlesham Heath aerodrome for test in about 1921.

It is, and was, an awkward-looking machine—a great, uncouth brute of a thing, but with a heart of gold. There were accidents with the Siskin as there were with all types used so extensively, but it was certainly an exceedingly safe machine. And now let me recall some of the performance figures.

The two most interesting Siskins in the series are the Siskin III with the Jaguar III engine and the Siskin IIIA, with the Armstrong Siddeley Jaguar IVS engine. The Siskin III was an aeroplane of moderate performance, capable of a speed not very much higher than that achieved by the war time Bristol monoplane, but carrying a greater load and two guns.

The maximum attained by the Siskin III was done at 6,500 ft., and was 134 m.p.h. At 10,000 ft. this machine did 133 m.p.h., and at 15,000 ft. it did 128 m.p.h. The ceiling was 20,500 ft. The climb to 6,500 ft. took 5 minutes ; to 10,000 ft., 8 minutes 36 seconds, and to 15,000 ft. 16 minutes 20 seconds. These figures were not outstanding, and it may seem curious that the machine was accepted so long after the war for use in quantity. But there can be little doubt that the need for performance was not fully realized at this period, and there was a slackening off in the effort to obtain performance with an increase in the effort to obtain comfort and load.

But with the introduction of the supercharged Jaguar IVS the Siskin's performance showed a considerable brightening up. At 6,500 ft. the speed was 154 m.p.h. The ceiling went up to 27,000 ft. and the climb to 6,500 ft. took 4 minutes 6 seconds, to 10,000 ft., 6 minutes 21 seconds, and to 15,000 ft. 10 minutes 36 seconds. There was an intermediate Siskin III whose speed was rather below this but which was better than the Siskin with the Jaguar III engine.

I have mentioned that the Siskin was used for racing. On two occasions—in 1923 and in 1925—the Siskin, with Armstrong Siddeley Jaguar engine, won the King's Cup. In 1923 it was entered by Mr. J. D. Siddeley, who is now Lord Kenilworth, and flown by Captain F. T. Courtney. The average speed stood as the highest at which the race had been won for five years.

In 1925 Mr. F. L. Barnard, the Imperial Airways pilot, flying a Siskin entered by Sir Eric Geddes, won the race at an average speed of 141 m.p.h. The race was a two-day affair, and Mr. Barnard went through dense fog on parts of the course and poor visibility over the whole course on the first day. In fact this race will be remembered for the remarkable address shown by Mr. Barnard in piercing bad weather and maintaining a true course.

The Siskin was also used for aerobatic demonstrations at the Royal Air Force Display and on many other occasions. Captain Courtney was one of the first to demonstrate the upward spin, or upward roll, in Great Britain, and he did it with a Siskin. He later showed the manœuvre in public at the Lympne light aeroplane competitions.

Tied-together drill, with a flight of three aeroplanes performing in unison, with their wing-tips linked by lengths of elastic cable, was originally developed with Siskin aeroplanes, and the race for the trophy presented by Sir Philip Sassoon for competition in the Royal Air Force was also won by a pilot in a Siskin on the last occasion on which the competition took the form of a race.

The Siddeley Siskin is difficult to place in the history of military development ; but it may be that it will eventually be shown to be one of the transitional machines from the war conception of the single-seater fighter to the peace conception of that type. Although externally it was not prepossessing according to the present-day standards, it incorporated many improvements and developments which have since proved to be of value.

THE F.2A FLYING BOAT

(See Frontispiece)

Yet another early machine which foreshadowed the future with a certain amount of authority and incorporated many ingenuities of design, was the F.2a flying boat. It is true that the biplane wing cell type has been superseded ; but the general conception of the flying boat, as such, stands and is accepted to-day. Among the F.2a's points of special interest were its opposite-handed engines.

Leonard Bridgman's drawing shows that the hull in general line conforms to present-day ideas in some respects ; but its mode of construction was entirely different, and there were differences in other important respects. The bottom of the hull was double-planked and the top was, at first, fabric-covered, the structure being of wire-braced wood and fabric. Later on the fabric top to the hull was changed for plywood covering. But the F.2a always brought together the boat type of construction and the aeroplane type of construction, and consequently it may be said to have marked a transition period in the development of marine aircraft ; a time at which the actual change was taking place between the land aircraft and the sea aircraft, and during which the structural methods of the boat and the aeroplane were found merged together.

The engines were Rolls-Royce Eagles and, as I have mentioned, they were originally arranged to run in opposite directions so as to cancel out torque effects. This was at first regarded as an essential for this type of machine ; but subsequently the America boats used engines running in the same sense and, as there were no marked ill-effects, this scheme was adopted and became general. Curiously enough, in 1938 the value of opposite-handed engines in twin-engined machines is again being emphasized, and in the United States of America their use is being advocated. So it seems that the F.2a may have been more prophetic than its designers thought.

The enclosed pilot's cockpit can be noted in Leonard Bridgman's picture, and the front and rear gunners' positions with their twin Lewis guns. There were also side gun positions in this flying boat. The wing tip floats are also to be noted, for they are a feature to which British designers have ever since been faithful in spite of the strong case made out by Dr. Dornier for stub floats. Even in the latest commercial monoplane flying boats, the wing tip floats are used for obtaining lateral stability on the water in preference to all other systems.

The wings, which spanned 86 feet, were in three bays, and the tail-plane was raised above the end of the hull itself. These F.2a flying boats were used for sea reconnaissance and for anti-submarine patrol and were in reality the heavier-than-air competitors of the blimp airships for this kind of work. They had a range of seven hours' flying which enabled them to undertake patrols of a kind which were out of the reach of other heavier-than-air craft.

In the biggest seaplane action of the war F.2as took part. On June 4th, 1918, five F.2as (two from Yarmouth and three from Felixstowe) set out to investigate enemy activity off the island of Texel. After one F.2a had been forced down with petrol feed trouble off Holland and duly interned, five enemy seaplanes turned up from Borkum and, after attacking the machine on the water and avoiding action with the other boats, one hostile aeroplane detached itself and returned to Borkum for help. The four F.2as remained circling round the crippled boat in case the enemy should return in force.

Three-quarters of an hour later a swarm of fifteen or sixteen enemy seaplanes arrived, and immediately they were seen Captain Leckie, the leader of the F.2as, signalled the flying boats to attack. In the meantime another F.2a had been forced to alight, and the remaining three boats in V-formation drove clean through the hostile force. Then followed a real " dog fight," with the great big five-and-a-half-ton flying boats being thrown about by their pilots, who had a most strenuous time.

The outcome of the action was that two F.2as were forced down, one with petrol feed trouble before the action began, and were finally interned in Holland. The enemy lost six fighting seaplanes. One F.2a was forced to alight on the water during the action owing to a broken petrol-pipe, but this was repaired and the boat was able to return home safely. The three F.2as returned to Yarmouth with only one casualty.

A remarkable and noteworthy fight this, waged right on the enemy's doorstep and three hours' flying from the British coast. Captain Leckie pungently reported after the action : " It is obvious that our greatest foes are not the enemy but our own petrol pipes."

As a result of this action it was decided that all flying boats should have their hulls distinctively painted for recognition purposes. Yarmouth pilots were allowed to paint their machines as they desired, and as a result the bizarre was not lacking. Felixstowe adopted a more systematic but no less striking system of painting, of which the accompanying illustration gives a notable example. The scheme of each individual boat was lettered and charts were prepared for issue to all air and naval units operating on the East Coast. All operational orders referred to these letters so that easy recognition by other aircraft and ships could be assured. This painting-up of the flying boats has nearly always been referred to as " dazzle-painting," whereas the object of it was exactly the opposite. The painting of the flying boats may have dazzled the enemy by its brilliance, but its primary function was to render the boats easily distinguishable by our own people.

The all-up weight of the F.2a was 10,978 lb., and I have it on the authority of Squadron Leader Maurice Wright, who was the test pilot who put these flying boats through some of their early trials, that they handled well and a good deal better than the bigger F.3 with its 103-ft. wing span. The petrol system, as has already been mentioned, was of interest. The fuel was carried in two separate tanks in the hull, and there were two wind-driven pumps which forced it up into a gravity tank and collector box in the centre section. From there it was fed to the carburetters. The top speed at 2,000 feet was 83 knots, and 3·8 minutes were taken to climb to that height. The air endurance was six hours and the service ceiling 9,500 feet.

Of aerodynamic interest, in the illustration, are the two fabric screens above the top plane. They occur where there are the king posts for bracing the wing extensions, and their purpose was to furnish additional fin area forward and high up to balance the fin area presented by the hull. Without these it was thought that the flying boat might easily become uncontrollable in a side-slip.

Essentially a British conception of the marine aircraft, the F.2a did a good deal to influence future flying boat design and to fix its direction. And in spite of the struts and wires, it cannot be said even now that the F.2a looks grossly old-fashioned.